Better Homes and Gardens®

COMPLETE GUIDE TO
QUILTING™

Better Homes and Gardens® Creative Collection™
Des Moines, Iowa

Better Homes and Gardens®
COMPLETE GUIDE TO
QUILTING™

Director of Editorial Administration	MICHAEL L. MAINE
Editor-in-Chief	BEVERLY RIVERS
Executive Editor	HEIDI KAISAND
Art Director	MELISSA GANSEN BEAUCHAMP
Senior Editor	JENNIFER ERBE KELTNER
Editor	DIANE YANNEY
Graphic Designer	MARY-BETH MAJEWSKI
Editorial Assistant	MARY IRISH
Contributing Graphic Designer	JANN WILLIAMS
Contributing Writers	JILL ABELOE MEAD, TERRI PAUSER WOLF
Contributing Copy Editors	DIANE DORO, JENNIFER SPEER RAMUNDT, MARY HELEN SCHILTZ
Technical Editors	LILA SCOTT, CINDY MARUTH, LISA FLYR
Proofreaders	ANGIE INGLE, MARCIA TETER
Photographer	PERRY STRUSE
Contributing Photo Stylists	JANET PITTMAN, CHRISTA BAHR
Contributing Quilt Designer	MABETH OXENREIDER
Contributing Technical Illustrator	CHRIS NEUBAUER GRAPHICS
Vice President Publishing Director	WILLIAM R. REED
Publisher	MAUREEN RUTH
Consumer Products Marketing Director	BEN JONES
Consumer Products Marketing Manager	KARRIE NELSON
Associate Business Director	CRAIG FEAR
Production Director	DOUGLAS M. JOHNSTON
Book Production Managers	PAM KVITNE, MARJORIE J. SCHENKELBERG
Marketing Assistant	CHERYL ECKERT

Meredith CORPORATION

Chairman and CEO	WILLIAM T. KERR
Chairman of the Executive Committee	E.T. MEREDITH III

Meredith Publishing Group
President	STEPHEN M. LACY
Magazine Group President	JERRY KAPLAN
Creative Services	ELLEN DE LATHOUDER
Manufacturing	BRUCE HESTON
Consumer Marketing	KARLA JEFFRIES
Finance and Administration	MAX RUNCIMAN

ISSN: 1540-9686   ISBN: 0-696-21512-8

For book editorial questions, write:
Better Homes and Gardens® Complete Guide to Quilting™ • 1716 Locust St., GA 205, Des Moines, IA 50309-3023

*L*ike having a trusted
quilting friend by your side. . . .

Whether you're a seasoned quilter or a novice who's always wanted to learn to quilt, this
one-stop, quilter-tested reference guide will show you, step-by-step, all you need to know.
We've included a variety of methods and techniques that will spark your creativity
and dozens of tips that will make quilting easier and more fun. This book will guide
you every step of the way—from buying supplies to sewing on binding and everything
in between.

The easy-to-use tabbed sections will make finding the answers to your questions
a breeze. The comprehensive index at the end of the book can be used to look up specific
references. Fill the pages at the end of each chapter with notes on things such as sewing
machine settings that work well for a particular technique, needle sizes you prefer, notes
from quilting classes you attend, or plans for your next quilt. In short, we hope that this
book develops well-worn edges from being used often over the years—helping to make
quilting even more satisfying.

A well-made quilt brings enjoyment to both the quiltmaker and the recipient. It's
our pleasure to provide you with proven methods that will help you spread the joy.

Happy quilting,

Executive Editor
American Patchwork & Quilting

Senior Editor
American Patchwork & Quilting

QUILTER
T E S T E D

FOR ACCURACY

O U R   P R O M I S E   T O   Y O U

Prior to publication we test every

technique shown to verify the accuracy

of our instructions. Then an experienced

team of editors reviews the text,

how-to directions, photographs,

illustrations, and charts to make sure

the information we provide you is

clear, concise, and complete.

The American
Patchwork & Quilting® Staff

Tools, Notions, & Supplies

1

TABLE OF CONTENTS
Chapter 1—Tools, Notions, & Supplies

QUILTER TESTED FOR ACCURACY

ONE OF THE JOYS OF QUILTING is that the supplies needed can be as simple as scissors, needle, and thread, or more complex with specialty tools designed for a specific purpose. There are literally hundreds of items to choose from to make quilting tasks easier, more accurate, or more fun. Whether you're a gadget-lover who wants every tool, or a minimalist looking to acquire the basics, knowing what the tools are, what to use them for, and why they're useful is essential to quilting success.

SCISSORS

Quilting requires a good pair of scissors. Most quilters use several pairs, each designed for a different purpose. Choose your cutting tools with care, making certain they are of the highest quality you can afford. It's better to have two or three sharp pairs of scissors than a drawer full of seldom-used, dull pairs.

Choose your scissors and shears from the following.

Thread clippers (A): Use for cutting threads. Single style used by both left- and right-handed persons.

Craft scissors and knife-edge straight trimmers (B): Use for cutting threads and trimming fabric edges. Left- and right-handed styles available.

Embroidery scissors (C): Use for thread cutting. Left- and right-handed styles available.

Appliqué scissors (D): Use for close trimming; special duckbill protects underneath layers of fabric. Left- and right-handed styles available.

Knife-edge bent trimmers or shears (E): Use for general cutting and sewing. Bent handle and flat edge provide accuracy when cutting on a flat surface. Left- and right-handed styles available.

Spring-action scissors (F): Small and large sizes available. Ideal for use by persons with weakened hands or for lengthy cutting sessions. Single style used by both left- and right-handed quilters.

> TIP: In a pinch with no scissors in sight? Use nail clippers to cut your thread.

ROTARY-CUTTING TOOLS

Although scissors are still often used for cutting fabric, the rotary cutter and mat board have revolutionized the industry and streamlined the process. To rotary-cut fabrics you need a ruler, mat, and rotary cutter (see Chapter 5—Cutting for information on how to rotary-cut).

ROTARY CUTTERS

Rotary cutters come with different types and sizes of blades and a variety of handle sizes. Try out the cutters before buying to find the grip and size that work for you.

A rotary cutter will cut through several layers of fabric at one time. Because the blade is sharp, be sure to purchase a cutter with a safety guard and keep the guard over the blade when you're not cutting.

Rotary cutters are commonly available in three sizes—28 mm, 45 mm, and 60 mm. A good first blade is 45 mm. The 28-mm size is good for small-scale projects, miniatures,

and corners. The 60-mm cutter can easily and accurately cut up to six layers of cotton fabrics.

Specialty blades, such as the 18-mm size, are used for cutting curves, miniatures, and appliqués; trimming seams; and cutting templates. Pinking and wave blades are used for novelty effects.

ACRYLIC RULERS

Accurate measurement is important for accurate piecing. To make straight cuts with a rotary cutter, choose a ruler of thick, clear plastic. Look for clear markings and accurate increments by measuring the ruler. Check to see if the 1" marks are the same crosswise and lengthwise.

Rulers come marked in a variety of colors. Try different rulers on cutting surfaces to see which is most easily visible for you.

There are rulers for every type of project and cutting need. Some rulers are almost like templates in that they create squares or right triangles in varying sizes. Some triangle rulers enable you to trim the points before joining the pieces together. If possible, try out rulers before you buy them or ask for a demonstration at a quilt shop and understand how to use them to get

SAFETY TIP: Rotary-cutter blades are extremely sharp. Develop a habit of retracting the blade after each cut. Just brushing your hand against an open blade can cause serious injury, as can dropping a rotary cutter with an open blade and striking your foot.

the maximum benefit from your purchase.

Rectangular rulers, such as a 6×24" ruler marked in ¼" increments with 30°, 45°, and 60° angles, are a good beginner's purchase. As you become more proficient you may wish to purchase additional acrylic rulers and templates in a variety of sizes and shapes.

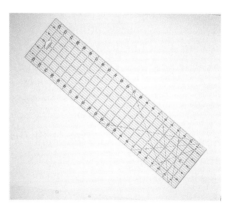

A good second ruler is the 6×12" size. It is easier to handle than the 24" ruler and can be used for smaller cuts and to make crosscut strips. It can also be used with the 6×24" ruler to cut 12" blocks or to make straightening cuts.

Square rulers, good for secondary cuts and cutting and squaring blocks, are available in a variety of sizes.

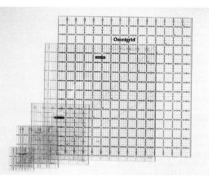

For squaring up large blocks and quilt corners a 12½" or 15½" square ruler works well. This ruler can also be used for making setting triangles.

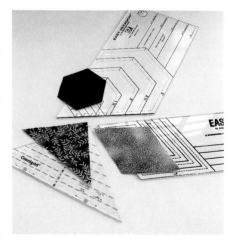

There are many rulers available that make cutting triangles, diamonds, and hexagons easy.

45° triangle rulers are useful for cutting half- and quarter-square triangles, mitering corners, and for cutting some diamonds and parallelograms.

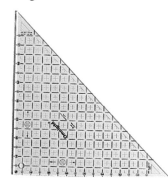

60° triangle rulers are helpful for cutting equilateral triangles, diamonds, and hexagons.

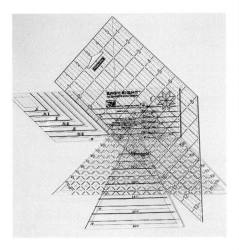

Specialty rulers and templates have been developed for cutting fans, arcs, Dresden Plates, Kaleidoscopes, some star patterns, and more.

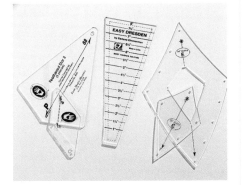

TIP: Have a project that calls for a specific size of square or rectangle? If the size is right, consider using a specialty triangle or square ruler instead of making a separate template.

Curved rulers and templates help cut Double Wedding Ring and Drunkard's Path pattern pieces.

ROTARY-CUTTING MATS

A rotary cutter should always be used with a mat designed specifically for it. The mat protects your work surface and keeps the fabric from shifting while you cut. Often mats are labeled as "self-healing," meaning the blade does not leave slash marks or grooves in the surface even after repeated usage. Many sizes, shapes, and styles are available, but a 16×23" mat marked with a 1" grid, hash marks at ⅛" increments, and 45° and 60° angles is a good first choice. For convenience, purchase a second smaller mat to take to workshops and classes.

Cutting mats usually have one side with a printed grid and one plain side. To avoid confusion when lining up fabric with preprinted lines on a ruler, some quilters prefer to use the plain side of the mat. Others prefer to use the mat's grid.

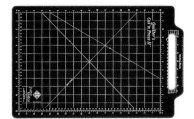

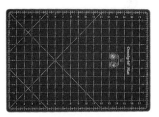

TIP: Due to possible variances between manufacturers, it's preferable to use one brand of ruler throughout a project.

Tools, Notions, & Supplies

Mats are also available with a mat board on one side and an ironing surface on the other side. This combination ironing board/cutting mat is great to have at workshops. Some mats have a lazy-Susan-type turnstile affixed underneath so you can swivel the mat easily. The smallest mat boards (less than 12") work well for trimming blocks while you are seated at the sewing machine.

Store cutting mats flat or hanging on a wall. To avoid permanent bends do not store a mat on an edge or rolled up. Heat will cause a mat to warp and become unstable, so keep all mats out of direct sunlight, don't iron on them unless they have an ironing surface, and never leave them in a hot car.

Periodically treat a mat to a good cleaning with warm (not hot) soapy water or window cleaner. Dry gently with a towel.

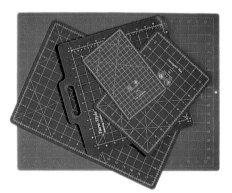

MARKING SUPPLIES

Many products are available for marking sewing lines and quilting designs on a quilt top. Useful supplies include fabric markers, templates, and pattern guides.

Variances in fabric contrast (light to dark) and fabric quality make marking different for each project, and a variety of markers may be needed for a single project. Try markers on fabric scraps and wash the test scraps as you will the quilt to be sure marks will wash out. Templates and pattern guides will vary according to the needs of each project.

FABRIC MARKERS

Artist's pencil: This silver pencil often works on both light and dark fabrics.

Chalk pencil: The chalk tends to brush away, so it is best to mark as you go with these pencils.

Mechanical pencil: Use hard lead (0.5) and mark lightly so that stitching or quilting will cover it.

Pounce: This is chalk in a bag. Pounce or pat the bag on a stencil, leaving a chalk design on the fabric. The chalk disappears easily, so mark as you go with a pounce.

Soap sliver: Sharpen the edges of leftover soap for a marker that washes out easily.

> **TIP:** With any marking tool work with a sharp point to get a fine, yet visible line.

Soapstone marker: If kept sharp, these markers will show up on light and dark fabrics.

Wash-out graphite marker: Keep the sharpener handy for these markers that work well on light and dark fabrics.

Wash-out pen or pencil: These markers maintain a point and are easy to see. Refer to the manufacturer's instructions to remove the markings and test them on scraps of your fabric to make sure the marks will wash out. *Note:* Humidity may make the marks disappear, and applying heat to them may make them permanent.

TEMPLATES AND PATTERN GUIDES

A template is a pattern made from extra-sturdy material so you can trace around it many times without wearing away the edges.

Quilting stencils and templates: Precut stencils and templates in a variety of shapes and sizes are available from quilt shops. These may be made from template plastic or a heavier-weight acrylic plastic. They can be traced around multiple times without wearing away any edges.

Some quilting stencils also are made from paper. They are designed to be stitched through and torn away after the design is completed.

Template plastic: Template plastic is an easy-to-cut, translucent material available at quilt shops and crafts supply stores. Its translucency allows you to trace a pattern directly onto its surface with pencil or permanent marker to make a stencil or template.

Test a variety of materials as some are heat-resistant (helpful when ironing over template edges) and some are not. Other varieties are gridded for accuracy in tracing or shaded for better visibility.

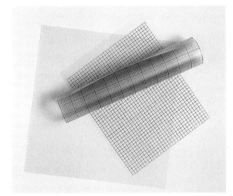

Freezer paper: Available at quilt shops and supermarkets, freezer paper allows you to create an iron-on template. You trace a shape onto the dull side of the freezer paper, cut

it out, and press it directly onto fabric with an iron.

Graph paper templates: You can use the printed lines on graph paper to draw a pattern piece. Glue the graph-paper pattern to template plastic, tag board, or cardboard. Allow the adhesive to dry before cutting through all layers at once to make an accurate template.

Clear vinyl: Also known as upholstery vinyl, this material is used by hand quilters to make overlays for accurately positioning appliqué pieces on foundation fabric (see Chapter 8—Appliqué for more information on the overlay method).

Tape: Several types of tape are used to mark quilting and stitching lines—quilter's tape, painter's tape, paper tape, and masking tape are

common choices. Quilter's tape is exactly ¼" wide; place it at the edge of your fabric and stitch alongside it for a ¼" seam allowance.

Specialty tapes in widths from ¹⁄₁₆ to 1" and wider are preprinted with lines to aid quilters in evenly spacing hand quilting or decorative stitches, such as a blanket stitch.

Some quilters use masking tape as a guide for straight-line machine or hand quilting. *Note:* Do not leave masking tape on fabric for an extended period of time as the adhesive from the tape may leave a residue. Painter's tape is less sticky than masking tape and also can be used as a guide for straight-line quilting.

THREAD AND NEEDLES

Thread and needles are at the heart of quilting as the two elements that literally hold everything together. Choosing the right type and size needle and thread can make a big difference in the success of your quilting project. Follow three general guidelines: match the thread type to the fabric fiber content, select the needle type based on the fabric being used, and select the needle size to match the thread.

TROUBLESHOOTING TIP: Can't see the lines of your ruler on the fabric? When working with dark fabrics, choose a ruler with yellow or white markings. For light fabrics, choose one with black markings.

TIP: Before working on your project, do a test to see how the thread and needle combination works. Sew together long strips of fabric to test piecing, or appliqué a patch. Create a little quilt sandwich (top, batting, and backing) and evaluate your quilting stitches.

TIP: The fabric strength should be greater than that of the thread used for piecing. If seams are under stress, the thread will then give way before the fabric tears. For this reason, strong polyester threads should not be used for piecing cotton fabrics.

Thread has multiple roles, from holding together patchwork to anchoring the fabric to the batting. Thread also plays a role in decoration, adding color, design, and texture to the quilt surface.

For piecing and most quilting, it's best to match the thread fiber to the fabric. Since most quilters use cotton fabric, 100% cotton thread is the best thread choice. Cotton thread is equal in strength to cotton fabric and should wear evenly. Synthetic threads, such as polyester, rayon, and nylon, are quite strong and can wear cotton fibers at the seams. For decorative quilting or embellishing, threads other than cotton may be appropriate (see Chapter 13— Specialty Techniques). Be sure your thread choice is suitable for the task; thread made for hand quilting, such as glazed cotton thread, should not be used in your sewing machine.

TIP: Typical thread weights are 30, 40, 50, 60, and 80. If the number of plies is equal, the higher number indicates finer thread. For example, a 50-weight three-ply thread is finer than a 40-weight three-ply thread.

THREAD TYPES

100% Cotton

Cotton thread is a staple in quilting. This thread works well with cotton fabric and is strong enough to create pieces that are durable. Hundreds of color choices are available in a variety of weights, although not all weights are created equal. Most cotton threads are two- or three-ply (see *page 1–8* for information on ply).

Cotton-Wrapped Polyester

Wrapping cotton around a polyester core creates a stronger thread with the finish characteristics of cotton thread. This thread is best used with fabric blends because it provides a little stretch. It's important to use a needle with a large eye to prevent stripping the cotton wrap from the polyester core.

Bobbin-Fill or Lingerie

Made from polyester or nylon and available in black or white, bobbin-fill works for machine embroidery, machine appliqué, or other decorative thread projects where multiple colors might be used in the needle. Prepare several bobbins filled with this thread and you can sew continuously without stopping to refill a bobbin. This thread is lighter weight than 100% cotton thread, which will cause the top thread to pull slightly through to the back side of the piece. Bobbin-fill is a more economical alternative to filling bobbins with specialty threads.

Metallic

The sheen and variety of colors available make metallic threads appealing for decorative stitching. However, metallic threads have a tendency to fray and break more often than cotton thread.

Using the right equipment will make the sewing process smoother. Work with a metallic or large-eye needle and a lightweight polyester, rayon, or nylon thread in the bobbin. Depending on your sewing machine manufacturer's specifications, you may also add liquid silicone drops to the spool to make the thread run through the machine more easily.

Monofilament

Available in clear or smoke color, this synthetic, lightweight thread comes in nylon and polyester. It generally is used for machine quilting when you don't want the quilting thread to show or where thread color may be an issue (i.e. quilting on multicolor prints). In the bobbin, use a lightweight cotton thread or bobbin-fill in a color that matches the backing.

TIP: Thread marked 50/3 (50 weight and 3 ply) works for both hand and machine quilting on cotton fabric. It's considered a medium-weight thread.

Perle Cotton

Soft and yarnlike, perle cotton is used for needlework projects or quilt embellishment. Typical weights used in quilting include Nos. 3, 5, 8, and 12. The higher the number, the finer the thread.

Polyester

This thread is designed for sewing with knits because the filament has the same stretch as knit fabric. Polyester thread should not be used with cotton fabrics for piecing or quilting, because it can be abrasive to soft cotton fibers and cause the fabric to tear at the seams.

Rayon

The soft, lustrous characteristics of rayon thread and the hundreds of colors available make it ideal for embellishment. It's often used for decorative quilting or embroidery. This thread is not strong enough and doesn't wear well enough to be used in piecing a quilt and should

be alternated with a cotton thread when quilting a project that will get lots of wear.

Silk

Silk thread is stronger than cotton because it is a continuous filament, unlike cotton's short, spun fibers. Silk also has more stretch than cotton thread. Some quilters prefer to use silk thread for hand appliqué because it glides through the fabric more easily than cotton and is usually finer, thus making it easier to hide the stitches. It also is less prone to fraying, allowing a longer length of thread to be used.

Variegated

This term applies to thread in which the color changes back and forth from light to dark throughout the strand or revolves through a range of colors to create a rainbow effect.

TIP: Choosing a Thread Color

Match thread and fabric colors when you want the quilting design to blend in with the quilt top or backing, such as when stippling or quilting in the ditch (see Chapter 11— Hand & Machine Quilting).

When you want to accentuate the quilting, choose a thread color in contrast to the fabric color. This may be especially important when using decorative threads as a strong design element.

TROUBLESHOOTING CHECKLIST FOR THREAD BREAKAGE

If you're having trouble with thread breaking, check these possible causes.

- **Damaged or incorrect needle:** Change the needle, as it may have dulled from overuse or could have a burr or nick. If the needle is new, check that it is the correct size and the eye is large enough for the thread type and weight being used (see the Thread and Coordinating Machine-Needle Sizes chart on *page 1–9*).

- **Defective or old thread:** Lower-quality threads may have thick and thin spots that lead to breakage. Thread that is too old becomes dry and brittle as it ages, causing it to break easily.

- **Improperly threaded machine:** Check to see that your spool is properly positioned on the sewing machine. The thread may be getting caught on the spool cap end as it comes off the top of the spool. The solution may be as simple as turning over the spool on the spool pin.

  Or, if the presser foot wasn't raised when you threaded the machine, the thread may not be caught between the tension discs inside the machine. The quickest fix is to remove the spool and rethread your machine with the presser foot raised.

- **Operator error:** Pushing or pulling on the fabric or allowing drag to be created by hanging a heavy quilt over your work surface can increase stress on the thread and cause breakage.

- **Tension too tight:** Refer to your machine's manual and *page 1-19* to determine if this is the cause of your thread breakage.

- **Wrong thread:** You may have the wrong thread type for the fabric you've chosen. Change thread and sew on a scrap of fabric to see how a different thread performs.

It is available in both cotton and rayon.

Water-Soluble

This thread dissolves in water. Use it to baste a quilt or anchor trapunto or reverse appliqué. Once the project is completed, immerse it in water to dissolve the thread. Be sure to store the thread in a dry, humidity-controlled location.

THREAD FINISHES

After thread is made, finishes are often added to enhance its ability to perform under certain sewing conditions.

Mercerized Cotton

Mercerization enhances the dyeability, increases the luster, and adds strength to cotton thread. Mercerized cotton thread is often used for machine piecing and quilting.

Glazed Cotton

Glazed cotton threads are treated with starches and special chemicals under controlled heat, then polished to a high luster. The glazing process results in a hard finish that protects the thread from abrasion. Glazed cotton thread is used for hand quilting; it should not be used in a sewing machine.

Bonded Threads

These are continuous-filament nylon or polyester threads that have been treated with a special resin to encapsulate the filaments. The resultant tough, smooth coating holds the plies together and adds significantly to the thread's ability to resist abrasion.

THREAD QUALITY

Buy the highest quality thread you can afford for your projects. Skimping in the thread department can create frustration with breakage, bleeding, and other problems. Consider the total cost of your quilting materials and your time, and know that saving a dollar on a spool of thread may not be worth it in the long run.

Cotton thread is made from cotton fibers, which are only as long as what the plant produces. The fibers are spun into a yarn and yarns are twisted into a thread. Poor quality threads are made from the shortest fibers and appear fuzzy along the length of the thread. They tend to fray and break easily. Higher quality threads are made from

longer fibers of cotton and have a smoother finish.

Ply

Thread is made from yarns that are twisted together into a single ply yarn. Plies are then twisted together to produce two-ply or three-ply threads, which are the kinds most commonly used for piecing.

Filament

This term is generally applied to man-made threads, such as polyester, nylon, or rayon, created from a chemical spinning process where a single strand or "filament" is produced. Silk is the only naturally occurring filament. Polyester and nylon threads are quite strong and are not normally used for piecing cotton since the fabric will tear before the thread breaks.

NEEDLES

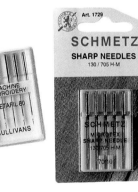

Whether you sew by hand or machine, using the correct needle size and type will make the task easier and the results more polished.

Machine- and hand-sewing needles have some similarities, but be aware that once you've mastered the numbers for machine-needle sizes, you'll need to learn a whole new set for hand-sewing needles.

> **Choosing a bobbin thread? For general piecing and quilting, use the same type of thread on the bobbin as is in the top of the machine (except with metallic or decorative threads). Trying to save money by using a less expensive or different type of thread on the bobbin can lead to tension difficulties.**

TROUBLESHOOTING TIP:
If you experience problems with breaking or twisting thread, the cause may be a needle mismatched to the thread type.

It is important to change needles frequently as both kinds become dull with use. If a machine needle strikes a pin or the machine bed, it can develop a nick or burr that can tear your fabric.

SEWING-MACHINE NEEDLES

The notions wall in your local quilt shop or sewing center can be intimidating if you're not sure what you need. There are dozens of sizes and shapes of sewing-machine needles, each designed for a different task. Understanding the terminology associated with machine needles can take the mystery out of making your selection and make your piecing and quilting go smoother.

Change needles at the start of a project and/or after 8 hours of sewing.

MACHINE NEEDLE SIZES

When looking at a package of machine needles, you will often see two numbers separated by a slash mark. The number on the left of the slash is the European size (range of 60 to 120); the right-hand number is the American size (range of 8 to 21). Sizes 70/10, 80/12, and 90/14 are most commonly used for quilting. A lower number indicates a finer machine needle.

MACHINE NEEDLE POINTS

The needle point differentiates the type and purpose of a needle and is a key characteristic to consider

ANATOMY OF A MACHINE NEEDLE

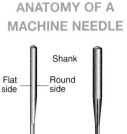

Shank | Flat side | Round side | Shaft | Groove | Scarf | Eye | Point | SIDE | FRONT

Shank: the part of the needle that goes into the machine.

Shaft: the body of the needle that extends below the shank.

Front Groove: the indentation on the front of the needle that allows the thread to lie close to the needle as it runs toward the bobbin. A deeper front groove can protect heavier thread from excess friction.

Scarf: the indentation on the back of the needle where the stitch is formed. When the bobbin shuttle swings into the scarf, it hooks into the looped thread on the needle to form the stitch.

Point: the tip of the needle. Select the point size based on the fabric being sewn.

Eye: the hole the thread passes through. Select the eye size based on thread type and weight.

THREAD AND COORDINATING MACHINE-NEEDLE SIZES

	60/8	70/10	75/11	80/12	90/14
Piecing and binding cotton fabric with cotton thread			●	●	
Piecing flannel					●
Quilting with monofilament thread	●	●	●	●	
Machine appliqué	●	●	●	●	
Sewing batiks, silks, or high thread-count fabrics with cotton thread		●			
Embellishing with decorative threads				●	●
Adding binding and borders			●	●	

when selecting a needle for a project. The needle point should match the fabric type. For sewing on quilting cotton, for example, use a needle labeled as a "sharps."

Needles last longer when the fabric and batting used are 100% cotton. Polyester or polyester/cotton blend batting tends to dull needles quicker.

> For machine needles, the larger the number, the larger the needle.

MACHINE NEEDLE EYES

A needle's eye must be large enough for the thread to pass through with minimal friction. If the eye is too large for the thread, it may produce a seam that is loose and weak. Large needles make large holes, so use the smallest needle appropriate for the thread. Some needles have eyes specially shaped for certain thread types, such as metallic threads, to minimize breakage (see the Thread and Coordinating Machine-Needle Sizes chart on *page 1–9*).

MACHINE NEEDLE TYPES

Sharps are the preferred needle type for piecing and quilting woven fabrics such as cotton. Sharps needles come in a variety of sizes and brands.

Universal needles can be used on both woven and knit fabrics but are not ideal for piecing because the needle points are slightly rounded. Choose this needle type if you want versatility when working with different fabrics.

Metallic needles are designed for use with metallic threads. A larger needle eye accommodates the thread, which tends to be fragile yet rough enough to create burrs in the eye of the needle. Burrs can cause the thread to fray and break.

Topstitch needles can handle heavier decorative threads but also leave larger holes in the fabric.

Specialty needles include double or triple needles, leather needles, and heirloom-sewing needles.

TROUBLESHOOTING CHECKLIST FOR NEEDLES
Your needle may be the culprit if these problems crop up while you're quilting.

- **Bearding** refers to the little white dots you see where your stitches come through the fabric. It occurs when batting comes through your fabric. Often the problem is caused by using too large a needle, a dull needle, or a needle that has a burr or nick.
- **Noisy machine stitching** (a sort of popping sound each time the needle pierces the fabric) is almost always a sign of a dull needle or damaged needle tip.
- **Skipped stitches** can be caused by a damaged or dull needle. If the needle is new, check to be sure it was inserted properly in the machine. Another problem may be a needle that is too small for the thread type. If the needle is too small, its front groove may be too shallow to protect the thread, causing stitches to be skipped.
- **Thread shredding** occurs for several reasons. The needle eye may be too small for the thread weight. If you have difficulty pulling the thread through the needle with ease, choose a needle with a larger eye. If you're hand quilting, you may have begun with a length of thread that's too long. If so, the thread may have become worn from being pulled through the fabric and batting too many times. If you're working with a metallic thread, be sure to use a metallic needle specifically designed to diminish thread shredding. Metallic needles have a larger eye to reduce the friction and heat caused by the speed of the machine needle piercing the fabric.

HAND-SEWING NEEDLES

Make hand sewing easier by selecting the right needle. Myriad hand-sewing needles are available through quilt shops and fabric stores. Understanding the type, size, and uses of each needle will help you select the one most suitable for your project.

HAND NEEDLE SIZES

A hand needle's size is determined by its diameter. There are two ranges in diameter size: 1 to 15 and 13 to 28. The diameter of a specific size remains consistent across the various needle types. In each case,

the larger the number, the finer the needle; all size 12 needles are finer than size 8, for example.

HAND NEEDLE POINTS

Hand-quilting needles have a sharp point that pierces fabric readily. Working with a dull needle can be frustrating and produce less

> **TIP:** For hand-sewing needles, the larger the number, the smaller or finer the needle.

HAND-SEWING NEEDLES

SMALL ROUND EYES	TYPE	LENGTH / DIAMETER	SIZES	USES
#8 Sharps	SHARPS	Medium / 41–76 mm	4–12	Hand piecing; general sewing; fine thread embroidery; sewing binding
#8 Betweens	BETWEENS/ QUILTING	Short / 41–76 mm	4–12	Hand piecing and quilting; appliqué; sewing binding
#9 Straw	STRAW/ MILLINERS	Long / 53–76 mm	4–10	Basting; gathering; appliqué
#8 Glovers	GLOVERS	Medium with a triangular point / 86–102 mm	1–3	Leather
		53–76 mm	4–10	Leather
LONG NARROW EYES				
#8 Embroidery	EMBROIDERY	Medium / 53–102 mm	1–10	Wool thread embroidery
#9 Darners	DARNERS	Long / 46–102 mm	1–11	Basting; weaving; tying comforters
		127–234 mm	14–18	
#9 Long Darners	LONG DARNERS	Double long / 61–183 mm	1–15	Weaving; tying comforters
#10 Beading	BEADING	Double long / 25–46 mm	10–15	Bead and sequin work
LONG OVAL EYES				
#26 Chenille	CHENILLE	Medium / 61–234 mm	12–26	Heavy thread embroidery; tying comforters
#26 Tapestry	TAPESTRY/ CROSS-STITCH	Medium with blunt point / 46–234 mm	13–28	Needlepoint; cross-stitch

Tools, Notions, & Supplies

desirable results. Just as with machine sewing, switching to a new needle after several hours of sewing is optimal.

HAND NEEDLE EYES

Needles with small, round eyes carry fine thread (approximately equal in diameter to the needle itself) that slides easily through the fabric. Longer needle eyes accommodate thicker threads and yarns. The oval eye found in tapestry and chenille needles helps create an opening in the fabric for thick, sometimes coarse fibers to pass through. Use the smallest needle appropriate to the thread to minimize holes in your fabric.

HAND NEEDLE TYPES

Quilters have many different uses for hand-sewing needles—hand piecing, hand quilting, appliqué, embroidery, tying, and securing binding. The point of the needle, the shape of the eye, and the needle's length in proportion to the eye determine its type. Short needles are easier to maneuver in small spaces. For tasks that require long stitches or lots of stitches on the needle, like basting, weaving, and gathering, there are longer needles.

Betweens have a small, round eye and come in sizes 4 to 12. Betweens are short and made of fine wire, resulting in a strong, flexible needle that's ideal for hand quilting, appliqué, and sewing binding. This is the most commonly used needle for hand quilting.

Sharps have a small, round eye and come in sizes 4 to 12. They are used for hand piecing, appliqué, general sewing, embroidery work that uses fine threads, and sewing binding.

Straw, or milliners, needles come in sizes 4 to 10. They have a small, round eye and are very long. These needles are often used for basting, gathering, and appliqué.

Beading needles are extra long with long, narrow eyes. Available in sizes 10 to 15, these needles are used for embellishment, beading, and sequin work.

Chenille needles have a long, oval eye and come in sizes 12 to 26. A chenille needle is often used for heavyweight thread, embroidery, and tying quilts.

Darners have a long, narrow eye. This needle type comes in sizes 1 to 11 and is used for basting, weaving, and tying quilts. Darners are also available in finer sizes ranging from 14 to 18. Long darners (double long needles) come in sizes 1 to 15 and can be used for weaving or tying quilts.

Embroidery needles come in sizes 1 to 10 and have a long, narrow eye. They are most often used for embroidery work with thicker decorative thread and wool thread.

Experiment with different pins to determine which ones work best for your needs.

Extra-fine, or silk, pins have thin shafts and sharp points. These pins make a small hole and are easy to insert.

Glass-head pins allow you to press fabric pieces with pins in place and not melt the pins' heads.

Flat flower pins have heads shaped like flowers. The long shaft makes them easy to grab and helps the pins stay put in the fabric.

Appliqué pins range from ¾ to 1¼" in length. They are designed to securely hold work in place yet prevent the sewing thread from getting snagged with each stitch.

Safety pins are clasps with a guard covering the point when closed. Use safety pins that are at least 1" long to pin-baste a quilt. Choose stainless-steel pins that are rust-proof and will not tarnish. There are several devices, including a spoon, that can be used to help close the pins, preventing hand fatigue. In addition, there are curved basting safety pins that slide in place without moving the quilt sandwich.

Whether you like to hand- or machine-quilt, there are a variety of general sewing supplies that are handy to have around.

NEEDLE THREADERS

Whether handheld or a machine attachment, this device makes getting the thread through the needle eye easier. Try several models to see which works best for your vision and coordination skills. Keep one close at hand to prevent eye strain.

SEAM RIPPERS

Although quilters don't enjoy "reverse sewing," sometimes it is necessary to remove a line of stitching. A sharp, good quality seam ripper can make the task of removing stitches easy and cause the least damage possible to your fabric. Choose one that is sharp and fits comfortably in your hand.

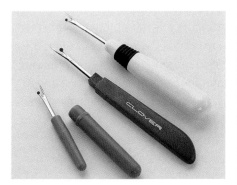

GRAPH PAPER

For pattern making or quilt designs use ⅛" (8 squares per inch) graph paper. If you're drawing a design on ¼" paper, enlarge the design on a copier by 400% to have a full-size copy. *Note:* Be sure to measure photocopies for distortion before using them as templates.

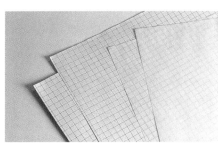

MEASURING TAPES

A measuring tape is essential for large measurements, such as border lengths or squaring up quilts. Make sure to purchase one that is long enough to cover your largest quilt measurement so you don't have to move the tape midway. Be aware that over time, a well-used cloth measuring tape may stretch and thus become inaccurate.

PINCUSHIONS

Pincushions are available in numerous styles, from the standard tomato shape so many of us are familiar with, to wrist, magnetic tabletop, and even decorative pincushions. Select a style that's easy for you to use. Some computerized machines may have problems with magnetic pincushions placed on or near the computer display screen. Check your machine manual for specific warnings.

The strawberry-shape needle cushion filled with emery that is often attached to a tomato-shape pincushion is an important aid in keeping your needles sharp and tarnish-free. Run all hand-sewing needles through the emery cushion before using them to remove any slight burrs, nicks, or residue.

STABILIZERS

Stabilizers are used beneath machine appliqué or machine embroidery work to add support to the foundation fabric, helping to eliminate puckers and pulling.

Stabilizers may be temporary or permanent. Temporary stabilizers are removed after stitching is complete. Permanent stabilizers remain in the quilt or are only partially cut away

---

CLASS OR WORKSHOP SUPPLY CHECKLIST
Use this list to be sure you have everything you need for a successful class.
- Supply list items specific to class (usually provided by instructor)
- Sewing machine with power cord, foot pedal, presser feet, and bobbin case
- Cutting tools
- Thread
- Bobbins
- Needles
- Scissors
- Needle threader
- Seam ripper
- Iron and pressing surface (unless provided)
- Extension cord
- Power strip
- Portable light

after stitching. Many brands are commercially available. Two of the most common types are tear-away and water-soluble. Freezer paper may also be used as a stabilizer.

Check the manufacturer's instructions on the package to select a stabilizer that is appropriate for your fabric and type of project. You may wish to experiment with a variety of stabilizers to determine which works best for you.

BIAS BARS

These heat-resistant metal or plastic bars may be purchased in a size to match the desired finished width of the bias tube you wish to make. They are a handy tool for making appliqué stems (see Chapter 8—Appliqué for more information on making bias stems).

REDUCING LENS OR DOOR PEEPHOLE

This device allows quilters to view fabrics and projects as if they are several feet away. Distance is valuable in determining design qualities (see Chapter 2—Fabric & Color for more information).

PRESSING EQUIPMENT

Proper pressing is essential to successful quilting. Even with the right equipment, understanding how to press can make a significant difference in the quality of your finished quilt. See Chapter 6—Hand Piecing and Chapter 7—Machine Piecing for information on how to press.

IRONS

Choose an iron that can be adjusted to a cotton setting and can be used with and without steam. There are a variety of irons available, including some small portable models that work well for classes or for special purposes, such as pressing bias strips or appliqués. If you plan to use your iron with fusible web, be sure to place a protective, nonstick sheet between your fabric and the iron to prevent the fusing adhesive from sticking to the sole of the iron. Or, consider purchasing a soleplate cover or second iron for use only with fusible web.

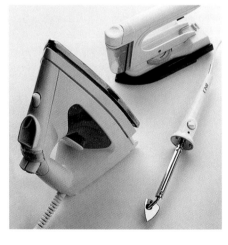

IRONING BOARD

Quilters have many choices in pressing surfaces, from the traditional ironing board with a tapered end to portable pressing surfaces/cutting boards in one. There are products available that allow you to create a pressing surface on a table, and there are large rectangular boards that fit over the traditional ironing board. The pressing surface can be covered with a purchased cover, or you can make one with batting and flannel or extra cotton fabric.

Do not choose a silver-color, teflon-coated cover for your pressing surface, as it reflects the heat, rather than allowing steam to pass completely through your fabric pieces.

STARCH AND SIZING

Some quilters like to work with fabric that has been starched, because they believe the fabric pieces are easier to handle and hold their shape better while pinning and stitching. Use a spray starch to add stiffening to prewashed fabrics or appliqué projects. Use spray sizing when more body but not as much stiffening is desired, such as when working with flannels. Wash the quilt after assembling.

ADHESIVES

BASTING SPRAY

Many brands of basting spray are available. The main point of difference is the ability to reposition the fabric. The sprays are often a good option for temporarily holding appliqués in place or for basting a small quilt or wall hanging together. Follow label directions and work in a ventilated area.

FABRIC GLUE

Fabric glue comes in several different forms. Whether you choose a type that comes in a bottle with a needle-tip applicator or a glue-stick version, important factors are making certain it is designed for use with fabric and is water-soluble and acid-free. When dry, fabric glue is more pliable than standard glue, and often its temporary bond allows you to reposition pieces without leaving permanent residue on your quilt.

FUSIBLE WEB

Available in prepackaged sheets or rolls, by the yard off the bolt, and as a narrow-width tape, fusible web is an iron-on adhesive that in nearly every case creates a permanent bond between layers of fabric.

Fusible web has adhesive on both sides with a paper backing on one side. It is most often used for machine appliqué.

The standard version for quilting is a lightweight, paper-backed fusible web specifically designed to be stitched through. When purchasing this product, check the label to make sure you've selected a sew-through type. If you are certain that you will not be sewing through the fused fabric (e.g. unfinished appliqué edges), you may wish to use a heavyweight, no-sew fusible web.

> **TIP: What is a BSK?**
> Basic Sewing Kit—You may see this abbreviation on class supply lists. Always bring along scissors, needles, and thread as part of your BSK.

The manufacturer's instructions for adhering fusible web vary by brand. Follow the instructions that come with your fusible web to ensure that you're using the correct iron temperature setting and know whether to use a dry or steam iron. These factors, along with the length of time you press, are critical to attaining a secure bond between the fusible web and the fabric.

BATTING

The material that goes between the quilt top and backing—batting—can vary from quilt to quilt. Learn the characteristics and properties of batting for the ideal match (see Chapter 10—Batting & Backing for complete information).

MACHINE QUILTING ACCESSORIES

Besides choosing needles and threads appropriate to your project, a couple other tools will make your machine quilting more successful. Personal preference dictates the use of many of the optional accessories.

QUILT CLIPS

Use quilt clips, or bicycle clips, to secure the rolled-up edges of a large quilt you are machine-quilting. These will help you better control the bulk of the quilt as you move it around while stitching.

WALKING OR EVEN-FEED FOOT

This foot evenly feeds multiple layers of fabric and batting for machine quilting, effectively providing feed dogs for the upper

fabrics to work in conjunction with the feed dogs on the machine bed. Some sewing machines come with a built-in dual-feed system, eliminating the need for a special foot. Other machines have brand-specific walking feet, while still others will accept a generic walking foot. (See Additional Accessory Feet on *page 1–19* for information on other specialty machine presser feet.)

HAND QUILTING ACCESSORIES

Beyond the all-important needle and thread choices that hand quilters make, there are few other tools required. Personal preference dictates the use of many of the optional accessories.

THIMBLES

Protect your fingers while quilting with a variety of thimbles. Choose

from metal or leather, or consider special pads that stick to your finger. Try them all to determine the style that works best for you. For difficult-to-fit fingers or simply increased comfort, custom-made thimbles are widely available.

QUILTING FRAMES AND HOOPS

Wooden hoops or frames are often used to hold quilt layers together, keeping them smooth and evenly taut, for hand quilting. The layers of a quilt should be basted together before inserting them into a hoop or frame.

Some quilters prefer hoops because they are smaller and lighter in weight than frames, take up less storage space, are portable, and can be retightened as needed.

Quilting hoops, which generally are sturdier than embroidery hoops, may be round, oval, square, or rectangular. Semicircular hoops, which are good for stitching borders or other areas close to a quilt's edges, are also available.

Hoops come in all sizes, but one with a diameter of 10 to 20" should be able to accommodate most quilting needs. Some hoops have a detachable floor stand that frees your hands for stitching and permits the hoop to be tilted and/or raised.

Most quilting frames consist of wooden top rails in a rectangular shape supported by sturdy legs.

They come in a wide range of sizes (30 to 120") so they can handle quilts up to king size. When using a frame, a quilt's edges are pinned or stitched flat to the rails so the layers are smooth, straight, and secure. One or both pairs of frame rails can be rotated to roll up the quilt and facilitate working on a small area at a time. A quilt frame must remain set up and in place until the quilting is complete.

WORK SPACE DESIGN FOR EFFICIENCY AND COMFORT

Although quilting may seem like a sedentary activity, it takes energy and the repetitive actions can stress joints and muscles. To keep sewing comfortably, follow a few simple tips for posture and position.

POSTURE

Be aware of your body posture. A straight back with your head and neck aligned and feet flat on the floor gives you the most support. Sitting or working at awkward angles and performing repetitive motions create situations that can cause injuries.

90 DEGREES

Keep this angle in mind whenever you sit down to perform a task.

Your back and legs should be at a 90° angle. Your upper and lower legs should form a 90° angle at your knees. When your feet are flat on the floor your ankles will also be at a 90° angle. Next look at your arms. Your elbows should be at a 90° angle with your forearms parallel to the work surface. Keep your elbows close to your sides and your shoulders straight.

TABLE OR LARGE WORK SURFACE

A large work surface allows you to lay out long yardages of fabric when cutting or to handle a medium- to large-size quilt for basting. In addition, a large surface can give you room to spread out a project for machine quilting, preventing the project from dragging or pulling, which can result in uneven stitches.

ADJUST THE WORK SURFACE

Once you have determined your 90° positions, raise or lower your work surface and/or chair in order to hold these positions and work comfortably.

If you raise your chair so your arms are at the work surface, you may not be able to keep your feet flat on the floor. Put a sturdy box or platform step under your feet so your knees and ankles stay at their 90° angles.

There are several products available at quilt shops and fabric stores that can adjust the tilt of your sewing machine or foot pedal to make it more comfortable to use and easier for you to see the machine bed. Many quilters find these products ease the stress and strain on their bodies when they sew for extended periods. If possible, sit down and try the products at the shop to see if they would aid in making your work space more comfortable.

Give yourself time. If you have been working at awkward angles, your body may have adapted and it may feel strange when you adjust your posture. Stay with the correct posture and you will benefit in the long run.

Align your cutting surface to hip height to eliminate the need to bend over and unnecessarily put strain on your back and shoulder muscles. If you're rotary cutting, use sharp rotary blades and rulers with nonskid material to decrease the amount of pressure needed to cut fabric, thus reducing the strain on your body.

When hand-quilting with a frame, it is best to first position your chair with your body at 90° angles. Next measure the distance between your elbows (bent at 90°) and the floor. Set the front roller bar of the quilting frame at this height, then adjust the back of the quilting frame.

DESIGN WALL

Having a vertical surface on which to lay out fabric choices can help you visualize how they might look in a quilt. For a permanent or portable design wall, cover foam core or board insulation with a napped material, such as felt or flannel, that will hold small fabric pieces in place. Some designers use the flannel backing of a vinyl tablecloth which can be rolled up between projects or hung on a hanger.

LIGHTING

Quilting requires overall lighting and nonglare directional lighting to avoid eyestrain and produce high-quality results. Review your quilting areas for lighting and invest in the appropriate fixtures to eliminate the headaches and vision problems that can result from eyestrain.

Several specialty lamps and bulbs specifically designed for quilters are available at quilt shops. Some are designed to more accurately reflect the colors of fabrics, filtering out excess yellow and blue tones that common household bulbs can cast. These can be especially helpful when you are selecting fabric combinations for your quilts and if your quilting area does not have abundant natural daylight.

WORKSHOP AND RETREAT SETUP

Plan for your posture and comfort needs when going to workshops and retreats. Bring your own portable table and chair, or anticipate the type of chair (often folding) and table (often portable and 30" high). Borrow a folding chair ahead of time and note your posture and the 90° positions. Use pillows or boxes to adjust your height, and take them to your class. Being properly positioned will allow you to be more productive and reduce the chances of developing pain in your joints and muscles.

KEEP MOVING FOR PERSONAL COMFORT

Though it's easy to get lost in your quilting, it is important to your overall health to pause for a few minutes every hour to step away from your sewing machine or quilting frame and stretch. If you take time to reposition yourself periodically, you can reduce muscle fatigue and eyestrain, and enjoy several hours of quilting. Speak with your health care provider about specific exercises that can help strengthen your neck, back, shoulders, arms, wrists, and hands.

CHECKLIST FOR HEALTHY QUILTING
- No reaching up to the work surface
- No hunching over
- No reaching over or out to the work surface (elbows at your side)
- Take 10-minute breaks every hour
- Drink extra water

SEWING MACHINES

Essential to machine piecing and quilting is the sewing machine. A serviceable, basic machine in good working order is sufficient for most purposes. Newer machines offer some features and optional accessories that make piecing and quilting easier and more enjoyable. Select a brand that can have its annual maintenance and repairs handled conveniently.

Understanding your machine's features can help you avoid problems or fix them when they arise. Your machine's manual is the best resource for specific information and problem solving. Some basic information applicable to most sewing machines follows.

HOW MACHINES STITCH

Two threads coming together to hold pieces of fabric in place may appear to be magic. In reality, it takes sophisticated engineering for the two threads to create straight and decorative stitches. Understanding how thread travels through the sewing machine can be useful in preventing and solving problems.

The seams created by machine are a series of lockstitches or knots. To create lockstitches on most machines, the thread runs from the spool through tension discs and into the take-up lever. As the needle goes down into the bobbin case, the take-up lever also moves down. In the bobbin case, the bobbin hook creates a loop that interlaces with the thread coming through the needle eye. As the take-up lever and needle come back up through the fabric, the loop formed with the bobbin and needle threads is pulled up to create a stitch.

SEWING MACHINE FEATURES

Only one basic function is needed to piece and quilt by machine—sewing straight, uniform stitches to create a seam that doesn't pucker or pull the fabric. Optional features may include some or all of the following.

Adjustable Stitch Length

This feature enables you to change your stitch length from long stitches for basting to tiny stitches you might use to secure your thread at the beginning or end of a seam or quilted area. In many newer machines, this feature is expressed in millimeters (10 to 12 stitches per inch equals a 2.0- to 2.5-mm setting). If knowing the stitches per inch is important to your project, create a sample swatch and measure the number of stitches in an inch.

Adjustable Stitch Width

This feature enables you to widen zigzag and other decorative machine stitches. It can be an important feature if you enjoy crazy quilting with decorative stitches (see Chapter 13—Specialty Techniques).

Zigzag and Satin Stitch

For a zigzag stitch, often used in machine appliqué, the needle swings from left to right. Adjusting the stitch length will produce stitches that are closer together. When the stitches form one against the other, filling any gaps, this creates satin stitching (see Chapter 8—Appliqué). Often the width of the stitch also can be varied.

Needle-Down Option

Once engaged, this feature allows the needle to stop sewing in the down position every time, allowing you to pivot or adjust the fabric without losing your stitching position. If disengaged, the needle will always stop in the up position.

> **READY-TO-SEW MACHINE CHECKLIST**
> - Machine in good working order
> - Foot pedal and machine plugged in
> - New needle in correct size for project
> - Correct presser foot
> - Bobbin wound
> - Threading done properly
> - Tension adjusted

Adjustable Feed Dogs

The ability to drop or cover the feed dogs is important if you want to do free-motion quilting (see Chapter 13—Specialty Techniques). When the feed dogs are in the up position, they grab onto the fabric as it moves under the presser foot.

With the feed dogs in the down position and a darning presser foot on, you can move the fabric freely on the machine bed, controlling where and at what rate the fabric feeds beneath the presser foot.

Easily Accessible Bobbin Case

When your bobbin runs out of thread, especially if you're in the middle of a project, being able to easily change or refill it is important. Look for a machine that offers easy access to the bobbin so that you don't have to take apart the machine bed or remove the machine from the cabinet.

Extended Machine Bed Surface

An extended surface is important if you do not have your machine in a cabinet with the arm in line with the cabinet surface and you're piecing or quilting large projects. Some portable machines come with a snap-on or slide-on tray that extends the bed of the machine. You may also purchase a surround that is customized to fit around the arm of your sewing machine to extend the work area. The larger, level work surface prevents the fabric from pulling and stretching under its own weight as you work with it.

Knee-Lift Presser Foot

This feature enables you to lift and lower the presser foot by pressing your knee on a bar that extends down from the machine front. It can be especially helpful when you need both hands free to hold your fabric.

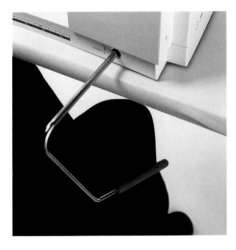

SEWING-MACHINE ACCESSORIES

Many machines come with a kit of standard accessories. Some have optional accessories you can purchase.

There are also a number of generic sewing accessories designed to work with a variety of machine models. Knowing your model brand and number when purchasing generic accessories is helpful, as the packaging often states the machines and brands with which the accessories will work.

Straight-Stitch Throat Plate

A straight-stitch throat plate has a small, round hole for the needle to pass through, rather than the larger opening of a standard throat plate. This smaller opening allows less area for the sewing machine to take in or "swallow" the fabric as it is being stitched and results in more uniform stitches.

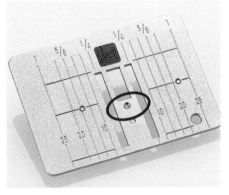

¼" Foot

Some machines allow you to reposition the needle so that it's ¼" from the edge of the standard presser foot. In addition, many machine models offer a special ¼" presser foot. With this foot and the needle in the standard position, the edge of the foot serves as the seam guide. For piecing, it is a useful accessory as you can watch only the edge of the fabric along the presser foot edge; you don't need to watch or mark a line along the throat plate or machine bed.

Additional Accessory Feet

An array of specialty feet, including open-toe appliqué and darning (used for free-motion quilting), cording, and binding feet, are available for a variety of machines. (See Machine Quilting Accessories on *page 1–15* for information on a walking, or even-feed, foot.) Check with your sewing machine's manufacturer for a complete list, or check the packaging of generic accessory feet to determine which models might be compatible with your machine.

(See Machine Quilting Accessories on *page 1–15*)

TENSION

When tension is balanced, stitches appear on both sides of the fabric without loops, surface knots, or broken thread.

For most piecing, your machine's tension will not need to be adjusted. Tension problems tend to be more prevalent when you're sewing with fabrics of different weights, heavy or decorative threads, or specialty needles. As with all sewing machine

> Knowing what affects the tension on your particular machine is critical for professional results.

adjustments, check your machine's manual first when attempting to solve a tension problem.

ADJUSTING UPPER THREAD TENSION

When a "bird's nest" of thread appears either on top of or underneath your fabric, the likely culprit is your upper thread tension. To determine what to correct, follow these guidelines:

If loops appear on the underside of the fabric, the upper thread tension may be too loose.

If knots appear on top of the fabric, the upper tension may be too tight.

Before adjusting the machine's tension dial, check to be sure your machine is properly threaded. If the presser foot was lowered as you were threading your machine, it is likely the upper thread is not between the tension discs inside the machine. Or, you may have missed one of the tension guides or the take-up lever. Simply raise the presser foot and rethread your machine.

If the problem still occurs, you may need to adjust the upper tension dial. If your tension is too tight, adjust the dial to a lower number to loosen it. If the upper thread tension is too loose, adjust the dial to a higher number to tighten it. Refer to your machine's manual for specific instructions about making tension dial adjustments.

ADJUSTING BOBBIN THREAD TENSION

Although many machines allow you to adjust the upper thread tension, the bobbin thread tension is generally set by the machine's manufacturer. It doesn't usually need to be adjusted unless you're working with decorative or specialty threads (see Extra Bobbin Case, *opposite*).

If your bobbin thread is knotting up on the underside of your fabric, try removing the bobbin and reloading it, making sure to properly insert the thread through the bobbin tension slots as directed in your sewing machine's manual.

In some cases, you may need to try threading your bobbin thread through the hole in the bobbin case "finger" to increase the tension. Your machine manual will have instructions for this procedure if it is an option on your machine.

BOBBINS

For general piecing and quilting, use the same type of thread in the bobbin as in the top of the machine. Metallic and decorative threads are the exceptions (see *page 1–6*). Trying to save money by using a less expensive or different type of thread in the bobbin can lead to tension difficulties.

Use bobbins that are specifically designed for your machine.

There are two basic types of bobbin mechanisms. The first is a front-loading bobbin, in which a filled bobbin fits into a bobbin case that then snaps into the opening on the front of the machine.

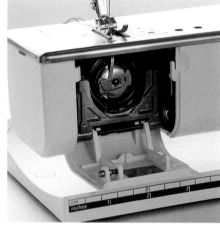

The second type of bobbin mechanism is the top-loading, or drop-in, bobbin. This type usually does not have a separate bobbin case. Instead, the filled bobbin simply drops into the bobbin casing in the bed of the machine, usually in front of the presser foot.

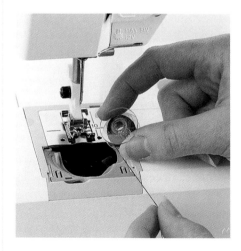

Winding Bobbins

For large projects, keep multiple bobbins filled by winding several at one sitting.

Follow your machine manufacturer's directions for bobbin winding. Be sure to start the thread in the correct direction and wind at a speed that allows for even filling. Winding your bobbin at too fast a speed can stretch the thread, resulting in a puckered seam.

Disposable, prewound bobbins are another option, depending on what your machine will accept and what your project requires.

Extra Bobbin Case

The bobbin case that came with your machine has been factory set for sewing with basic threads. If you plan to sew with specialty threads, consider purchasing an additional bobbin case (if your machine accepts one) for use with decorative or thicker threads.

You will need to adjust the tension for these threads by turning the screw on the bobbin case's tension spring. Turn it to the left to loosen the tension and to the right to tighten the tension.

For heavy, thick threads the tension generally needs to be loosened, and this should be accomplished in less than two complete rotations of the screw. Work over a bowl, box, or plastic bag in case the screw comes out.

Always sew a test sample after adjusting the screw.

Place a dot of nail polish or permanent marker on the second case to designate it as the case that has had its tension adjusted.

If you only have one bobbin case, make notes in this book or in your machine's manual to indicate changes in screw or tension settings when using different threads. For example, you might write "left 1½ turns for No. 5 perle cotton."

Tools, Notions, & Supplies

My Notes for Tools, Notions, & Supplies

Fabric & Color

2

TABLE OF CONTENTS
Chapter 2—Fabric & Color

FABRIC & COLOR

SELECTING JUST THE RIGHT FABRICS IN JUST THE RIGHT COLORS is part of the fun of quilting. For some quilters, however, this step in the quiltmaking process can be the most daunting. Understanding how your fabric and color choices affect the overall appearance of a finished quilt can help make the selection process easier.

FABRIC

Understanding how fabric is made and what kind of finishes are applied can help you select fabric for your project.

FABRIC MANUFACTURING BASICS

Most quilting fabrics begin as greige (gray-zh) goods, which means unbleached and undyed. Fabrics in this state must be cleaned and prepared before any color can be added or design printed. Greige goods can range in weave from loose to tight and their surfaces may have imperfections. The number of threads per square inch varies according to each manufacturer's specifications. Each of these characteristics affects the finished product's quality, durability, hand (or feel), and price.

Because manufacturers try to meet different market demands for products and prices, it's common for a manufacturer to print the same design on different quality greige goods. The fabrics may appear the same and have the same manufacturer and designer names

printed on the selvages, but may vary in terms of durability or quality.

Homespuns are one of the few fabric types that don't begin as greige goods. Instead, they are woven with colored threads.

PRODUCING A FINISHED PRODUCT

Color and design are dyed, screen printed, or roller printed onto greige goods. Occasionally dyed fabrics may be overprinted, meaning they are first dyed, then printed.

Finishes are added to greige goods through mechanical or chemical means and range from temporary to permanent. Permanent finishes, as the label implies, endure for the life of the fabric. Durable finishes lose some of their properties with each cleaning, but, with proper care, should last nearly as long as the fabric. Semidurable finishes will last through several launderings, while temporary finishes are lost after the first washing.

Many quilting cottons have a finish applied to reduce wrinkling. This is beneficial when you're working with a fabric, and is important to know as it may affect your ability to press seams flat by preventing the fabric from holding a sharp crease.

Fabrics with a polished appearance on one side have been glazed. The finish tends to wear off over time, but some quilters find it helpful during quiltmaking as it adds a stiffness to the fabric.

More loosely woven fabrics are sometimes finished with a process called napping, which creates flannel. The fabric runs over a series of napping rolls that raise the surface nap of the fabric. Fabrics can be napped on one or both sides.

Because of the looser yarns and weave required to create the nap, flannel fabrics tend to shrink more than other woven fabrics do.

Cotton fabrics with an especially soft feel may have had a mechanical sueding finish applied.

FIBER CONTENT

The preferred fabric fiber content for quilting is 100% cotton. However, even within this category, there are choices to make. Other fiber content options also are available.

100% Cotton

Cotton is woven in many ways to create a variety of products. Some of these products work well in quilts, and others are better suited for home decorating and garment making. Poplin, chino, chenille, and velveteen can be 100% cotton, for example, but may not work well for intricately pieced quilts.

Always consider the intended use when choosing quilting fabrics, as different fabrics behave in different ways when sewn, pressed, hung, or laundered. If you plan to combine different types of 100% cotton fabrics in a quilt, know that the

pieced units will only be as strong as the weakest fabric, and you may have to deal with such complications as puckering, sagging, and pulling.

Several types of 100% cotton fabrics are often used in quiltmaking. They include broadcloth or plain-weave cotton, homespun, flannel, and chintz.

Broadcloth or Plain-Weave Cotton:
This fabric, often called quilters' cotton, has several benefits, including a weight, or body, that allows it to be sewn with little slippage. It creases well, so seams open flat. It is durable and doesn't readily fray. It also will tear along the grain line. When used in bedding, cotton's natural fibers wick moisture away from the body, increasing comfort.

Homespun:
Already-dyed threads are woven into a solid, plaid, striped, or checked design for these fabrics. They are often used when a primitive look is desired.

Flannel:
This fabric is woven of a bulkier cotton thread with a looser fiber, then brushed to give it a nap.

Chintz:
A high thread count and glazed finish make this fabric more difficult to needle than other 100% cottons. It frequently puckers when stitched, and needles and pins may cause permanent holes.

Other Fiber Choices
Fabrics with a fiber content other than 100% cotton, including wool and silk, can be used in quilting, though it's best to stick with the same content within a single quilt.

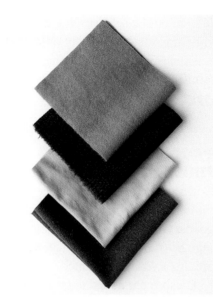

Wool: Working with wool offers quilters nearly as many options as working with cotton. Felted wool is especially easy to use in appliqué, as the edges don't need to be turned under since they will not ravel.

To felt wool, machine-wash it in a hot-water wash/cool-water rinse cycle with a small amount of detergent, machine-dry, and steam press. If you wish to use wool from a piece of clothing, cut it apart and remove the seams before washing so it can shrink freely.

Silk: This natural fiber has luster and can be smooth or have slubs (small threads) on the surface. Silk generally requires more care in cleaning than cotton does.

DETERMINING FIBER CONTENT AND THREAD COUNT
Check the Fabric Bolt End
The percentage of fibers is usually listed on the end of the fabric's cardboard bolt, along with information about special finishes, such as if the fabric is chintz or is permanent press. Care instructions,

style number, the fabric and manufacturer's name, and any processing, such as preshrinking, will also be noted.

Note: Some fabric stores rewrap fabric flat folds around unused cardboard bolts. Be sure to confirm that the information on the bolt end matches the manufacturer and fabric name on the fabric selvage.

Thread Count
The number of threads per square inch determines the quality and weight of a fabric. If the thread count is the same for both length and width, the fabric is said to have an even weave.

Quilting cotton has a higher thread count (68×68 threads per square inch) than lighter-weight cotton. Fabrics with low thread counts (less than 60×60 threads per square inch) are too lightweight to use successfully in a quilt, as they will ravel excessively when they are handled. Low thread counts also mean more shrinkage, less durability, and bearding (batting coming through the quilt top or backing). Pieces can fray and fall apart if seams need to be removed.

Higher thread counts and extremely tight weaves can be difficult to needle. It may be tempting to use a sheet for a quilt back, for example, but the finish and thread count make it difficult to work with and create puckering.

GRAIN LINE

Cutting pieces according to a fabric's grain line makes for more accurate piecing and a stronger finished quilt top. Following the grain line reduces stretching and distortion, enhancing the overall appearance of your finished quilt.

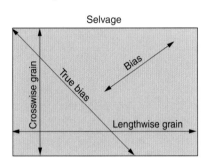

In weaving fabric, manufacturers place the lengthwise threads (warp) tightly in the loom to eliminate stretch. The crosswise (weft) threads are then woven into the lengthwise threads, but are not stretched as tightly, leaving a little "give" in the finished fabric.

Fabric pieces cut diagonally across the grain line, or on the bias, are susceptible to stretching because there are no stabilizing threads along the edges. If the design motif can only be cut on the bias, backing it with a lightweight fusible web can help to stabilize it.

RIGHT SIDE/WRONG SIDE

Most manufacturers print on one side of the greige goods. This means the fabric has two sides (right and wrong, or front and back). The back of the fabric, or wrong side, may have some color from the dye bleeding through. If you need a lighter shade of a fabric in your quilt, you may wish to use the "back" or wrong side of the fabric as the right side.

Batiks have very little difference between the right and wrong sides. Homespuns, which are woven from already-dyed threads, look the same on both sides.

SPECIALTY FABRIC CUTS

Two common specialty cuts of fabrics—fat quarters and fat eighths—are found in a majority of quilt shops. Many quilters find these sizes offer more versatility for cutting templates or strips than the actual ¼-yard and ⅛-yard cuts.

Fat Quarter

Although a traditional ¼-yard cut and a fat-quarter cut are the same amount of fabric, the difference is the shape. A traditional ¼-yard cut measures 9×44". A fat quarter is ¼ yard of fabric cut crosswise from a ½-yard piece of fabric—an 18×44" rectangle of fabric cut in half to yield an 18×22" "fat" ¼-yard piece.

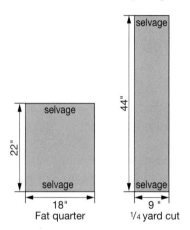

Fat Eighth

Although a traditional ⅛-yard cut and a fat-eighth cut are the same amount of fabric, the difference is the shape. A traditional ⅛-yard cut is 4½×44". A fat eighth is cut crosswise from a ¼-yard piece of fabric—a 9×44" rectangle of fabric cut in half to make a 9×22" "fat" ⅛-yard piece.

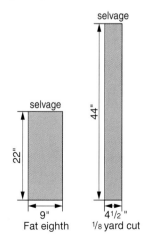

BEFORE YOU BUY FABRIC

Determine how much fabric you'll need for a project before you go shopping. Graph paper helps take out the guesswork.

Use graph paper to create a cutting diagram. Let each square equal 1" and map out the needed pieces. You may wish to purchase ⅛ to ¼ yard more fabric than your layout requires to allow for inches that may be lost in squaring up fabric edges, shrinkage during prewashing, and/or cutting errors.

Make template windows out of sturdy paper or cardboard to take to the fabric store for previewing fabric options. Do not include seam allowances in the window cut, but do leave a healthy margin of paper

around each window to help differentiate what's showing through from the rest of the bolt. Viewing a fabric through a template window can help you see what individual pieces look like more easily than looking at the whole bolt will.

Once you're in the quilt store or fabric shop, the array of colors and designs that fill the shelves can be both exciting and intimidating. When you're selecting fabrics for a project, consider the following suggestions:

Separate the bolts you're interested in from the other fabrics. Examine them away from other fabrics to avoid confusion or interference from other colors.

Stack the bolts horizontally to view how the fabrics may appear when cut into smaller shapes (if you don't have template windows) and how they work together.

Stand back about 10 feet and look at the bolts stacked horizontally. A view from this distance will give you an idea of how a fabric combination will work in a quilt.

Find optimum light. Fluorescent lighting can sometimes cast a yellow glow, altering the appearance of a fabric's true colors. Take the bolts to the area of the store that has the most natural light. Stand with the light at your back and let it wash across the bolts.

FABRIC PREPARATION

All fabrics are subject to loss of color from washing, exposure to light, and abrasion. Whether to prewash fabrics or not is a topic of much debate among quilters.

Many of those who don't prewash find it easier to work with fabrics that have the sizing and finish from the manufacturing process still on them. Others don't prewash because the shrinkage of the fabric after a quilt is complete can create the rumpled, old look of an antique that they desire.

Some quilters favor prewashing fabrics to reduce uneven shrinkage or colors bleeding once a quilt is complete.

Your decision about prewashing may change from one project to the next. Consider these color-retention factors when making your choice.

COLOR-RETENTION FACTORS

Whether you're prewashing fabric or laundering a finished quilt, several factors affect a fabric's ability to retain its color.

Hot water can be damaging to any fabric's color and finish. Cold water is safest for washing cotton. Check first to see if any color is released at this temperature by filling a clear

glass with cold water and dropping in a swatch of the fabric. If the water changes color as a result of dyes being released, prewashing the fabric will be necessary to rid the fabric of excess dye before using it in a quilt. After prewashing, retest a swatch in a clear glass to see if the dye-bleeding problem has been resolved.

Detergents can break down the binding agents that hold pigment on cloth. Detergents with chlorine bleach can damage fiber-reactive dyes. Gentle soaps and cleansers made specifically for cleaning quilts are widely available at quilt shops and some fabric stores.

As with any product, it is important to follow the manufacturer's instructions and use the correct amount. Soils remain if too little is used, and fabric is affected if too much is used and it's not rinsed out properly.

Abrasion, or the friction of fabrics rubbing against each other, may cause crocking, which is a transfer of color from one fabric to another. The friction may be caused by handling or from contact in the washer and dryer. Colors may leach out of a piece of fabric, causing a color loss in that piece, but the real concern is whether or not the dye will then permanently reattach itself to other fabrics.

If you are working with high-contrast fabrics, such as red and white, one method of testing for crocking is to pretreat the fabrics as desired, then vigorously rub them against one another. If any of the darker color rubs off on the lighter fabric, you must pretreat it again until the fabric passes the rub test.

Another test to determine if color will migrate from one fabric to another is to put the suspect fabric (usually a dark, intensely colored fabric) in a jar of water with 1 teaspoon of the detergent you might launder it in. Check for color loss after 10 minutes. If color is present in the water, add a piece of the light fabric to the water and shake the jar several times. Leave both fabrics in the water for 10 minutes, then remove the lighter sample and compare it to the original light fabric. If there is no transfer of color, the dark fabric should be safe to use even with color loss in the water.

FABRIC AND QUILT CARE

Caring for fabrics properly, both before and after they're sewn into a quilt, can increase their longevity. Whether your quilts are stored for a long period of time or are periodically rotated on display, follow these guidelines to protect them from fiber damage and keep them at their best.

SOURCES OF FIBER DAMAGE
Light
Fluorescent lights and ultraviolet radiation from sunlight cause fabric dyes to fade and fibers to become brittle. Rotate quilts frequently to prevent damage from exposure to light. Watch quilts displayed on beds, as the side exposed to sunlight from a nearby window may fade. Cover windows with shades when sunlight is direct. Make sure that quilts are not stored in an area exposed to direct sunlight to prevent the exposed portions from fading.

Folds and Creases
When folded fabrics or quilts are stored for long periods of time, the fibers along the folds begin to weaken, and permanent creases can develop. Some quilters refold their fabrics periodically to keep this from occurring. It's best to roll, rather than fold, quilts for storage, adding acid-free tissue paper between the layers of the quilt to help prevent creasing.

Acid
Paper, cardboard, plastics, and unfinished wood in shelves, drawers, and trunks release acid, which is damaging to plant-derived fabrics, such as cotton and linen. Prevent your fabrics and quilts from coming in contact with these surfaces by rolling them in acid-free tissue paper and storing them in acid-free boxes or white, cotton pillowcases.

TIP: Clean Hands Preserve Quilts
From the first cut of fabric to the last stitch of the binding, having clean hands and a clean work area will help preserve your quilt. Wash your hands often when working on a project and avoid contact with food and drink. Residues from the acids and salts on your hands and in food products may attract insects, which will cause damage. White gloves aren't only for quilt shows; use them when handling quilts that you want to preserve for generations.

Mold/Mildew

Mold and mildew flourish in warm, moist environments, so quilts shut in closed containers or wrapped in plastic and stored in areas of temperature extremes and excess moisture (attics, basements, garages) are susceptible to the growth of these fungi.

To avoid the irreversible damage caused by mold and mildew, and to protect your quilts from dust and other elements, store them in a cool, dry location (less than 50% humidity) wrapped in white, cotton pillowcases to allow air to pass through and let the quilts breathe.

Time

Antique fibers need to be handled with care. Vintage fabrics can be prone to damage by laundering. Unstable dyes and pigments, weave, and age make these fabrics especially sensitive to today's cleaning methods.

For example, some older fabrics were made with unstable dyes, and any contact with moisture may cause them to bleed. This is especially noticeable with brown and black dyes in antique quilts. Other fabrics become brittle with time and may turn to powder.

Contact an expert, such as a quilt preservationist or appraiser at a museum or university, for recommendations on handling, cleaning, and preserving older quilts.

CARING FOR QUILTS ON DISPLAY

Rotate the quilts on display often to give them a rest. This will diminish their exposure to dust, light, and other potential sources of fiber damage (see Sources of Fiber Damage, which begins on *page 2–5*, for more information).

A quilt that doesn't have an obvious top or bottom can be turned periodically to prevent distortion or damage to the fibers along one end. You may wish to add a hanging sleeve to more than one edge to make rotating the quilt easier. (See Chapter 12—Binding & Finishing for information on adding hanging sleeves.)

CLEANING METHODS

Avoid washing a quilt unless it's absolutely necessary. Washing, even when done on a gentle cycle, causes fabrics to fade and is abrasive to fibers. Clean and freshen a quilt using one of these methods.

Airing Outdoors

Annually take quilts outdoors on an overcast, dry, and windy day to be refreshed. Place towels or a mattress pad on the dry ground and lay your quilts on them. Cover the quilts with a sheet to prevent debris from falling on them. Avoid placing quilts on a clothesline to prevent stress on the seams.

Using a Dryer

Quilts can be freshened in a dryer on a gentle-cycle/air-dry setting without heat.

Vacuuming

Vacuuming both the front and back of a quilt can help preserve it by removing dust and dirt. Place a nylon hose or net over the end of a vacuum hose and gently draw the hose over the quilt's surface without rubbing it. You can also lay a piece of clean screening on the quilt, then vacuum it. Always clean a quilt with at least a quick vacuuming to remove airborne dust and dirt before storing it.

> **TROUBLESHOOTING TIP:**
> It's often too much time in an overly hot dryer that shrinks cotton fabrics unnecessarily, as most shrinkage happens near the end of the drying cycle, when the fabric is about 75% dry. If line-drying your fabrics isn't an option, remove them from the dryer when they're still damp and press them with a dry iron.

> **TIP:** Evaluate antique quilts individually before attempting to clean them. Improper cleaning can damage a quilt. If a quilt has sentimental or monetary value, consult an expert before attempting to clean it. Contact a quilt museum, university textile department, or antique expert for references.

Washing

As a last resort, cotton quilts can be washed in cold water with a gentle soap by hand or in the machine on a gentle cycle. Do not wring or twist a quilt; instead gently squeeze out the water. Wet quilts are heavy and need to be supported when you are moving them to a flat area to dry.

Washing by Hand

1. Use a clean tub that is free from other soaps or cleaning materials.

2. Place a large towel or cotton blanket in the tub to support the quilt.

3. Thoroughly dissolve soap in water prior to adding the quilt to the tub. Be sure you have enough water in the tub to cover the quilt.

4. Place the quilt in the tub. Gently agitate (do not wring or twist) the quilt to release the dirt and soil.

5. Rinse the quilt by draining and refilling the tub. Repeat as needed to remove soap, as residue can build up on a quilt's surface.

6. Press excess water out of the quilt, starting at the end farthest from the drain and working your way across the quilt. Use towels to blot up excess water.

7. Remove the quilt from the tub, using the large towel or cotton blanket beneath it.

8. Spread the quilt flat on a clean sheet that has been placed out of direct sunlight. Let it air-dry, using a fan to speed the process.

Washing by Machine

1. Fill the washing machine with water and dissolve the soap.

2. Place the quilt in the machine. Let it soak for up to 15 minutes, checking it frequently to make sure the fabric dyes are stable and not running onto neighboring fabrics. If desired, agitate the quilt on a gentle cycle for up to five minutes. *Note:* A front-loading washing machine will not allow you to soak the quilt in the washer drum. Agitating on a gentle cycle is necessary in this type of washing machine.

3. Repeat steps 1 and 2 with fresh soap and water if a quilt is especially soiled.

4. Use a gentle spin cycle to rinse the quilt and remove the excess water. Continue to rinse and spin until the rinse water is free of soap.

5. Remove the quilt from the machine and spread it flat on a clean sheet that has been placed out of direct sunlight. Let it air-dry, using a fan to speed the process.

Dry Cleaning

It is wise to check references before selecting a dry cleaner to handle your quilts, as dry cleaning can cause cotton dyes to bleed or change color.

Take special precautions if you wish to dry-clean a wool or silk quilt. Dry cleaning should be a last resort, used only if vacuuming or spot cleaning doesn't remove the soil.

TIP: An unused bed makes an ideal storage spot for quilts. Spread your quilts on the bed, separating them with layers of cotton fabric, cotton sheets, or batting to prevent any dye transfer.

DESIGN CONCEPTS

Use the three Cs when selecting fabrics for your quilt—contrast, color, and character.

Although color is fun and exciting, it is contrast, or differences in values, that often makes a design successful. Without contrast in value between pieces in a block or the blocks in a quilt top, the colors will blend together and the design itself may get lost.

It's important to choose colors that appeal to you and suit the design. A block design may work with odd colors that have good contrast, but it may not be as visually pleasing.

The character of the fabric, or its motif, also influences a quilt. Motifs can range from polka dots or stripes to florals, calicoes, novelty prints, plaids, and large-scale patterns.

SEEING DESIGN AT WORK

Different quilts and styles of quilting attract different quilters for different reasons. Before you select fabrics, it may be helpful to thumb through quilting books, magazines, and patterns. Note the common qualities among the quilts that attract your eye.

Do you like quilts with stark contrast between colors, such as a quilt composed solely of red and white? Are you attracted to scrappy

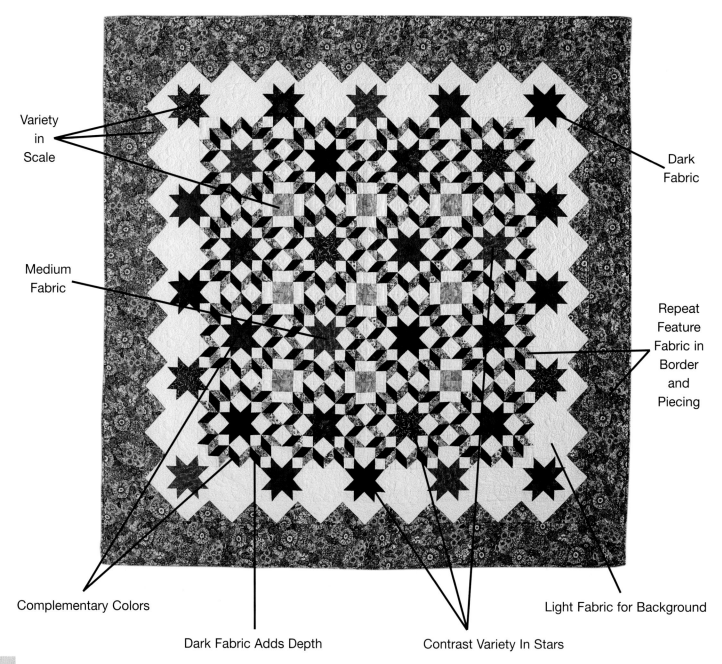

Variety in Scale

Dark Fabric

Medium Fabric

Repeat Feature Fabric in Border and Piecing

Complementary Colors

Dark Fabric Adds Depth

Contrast Variety In Stars

Light Fabric for Background

quilts with dozens of different fabrics included? Do you like quilts with muted tones where the colors seem to meld together?

Knowing what you like is the first step in selecting fabrics. For an idea of where to start, look at the quilt *opposite*. Study its design in terms of color, contrast, and character to learn how the fabric choices affect a quilt's overall appearance.

This quilt provides a good example of how to use a range of light-, medium-, and dark-value fabrics in a composition. The light background brings out the lighter colors in the other fabrics, while the light-color shapes and images in the quilt center appear to come forward.

The dark fabrics appear smaller in the overall quilt design. The dark shapes and images seem to recede, adding depth to the design.

The medium fabrics are a mix of light and dark colors, eliminating the possibility of a blended or flat design. The floral print used in the rings that surround the stars is repeated in the border, giving the quilt continuity. Its large-scale print also adds nice balance to the small-scale light and dark prints.

CONTRAST (VALUE)

One of the first design concepts to consider when composing a quilt is contrast. Many quilt patterns list the fabrics needed for a project in terms of their contrast or values—light, medium, or dark. Learning to see fabrics in these categories of contrast can enhance your fabric selection success.

WHY CONTRAST?

Contrast clarifies the design and makes depth apparent. Without contrast between the medium gold and the medium green in the block *below*, the pieces in the block blend together, and the design appears flat.

The shapes take on new dimensions when the fabrics—a dark purple, medium green, and light yellow—have more contrast.

TIP: Fabric manufacturers tend to produce more fabrics in the medium range. When you see light or dark fabrics that you like, add them to your stash.

Contrast, however, is a relative concept. The block *below* uses a medium-value purple for the center star and a darker purple for the background. Because there isn't too much difference between the medium and dark values, the contrast in the resulting block is subtle.

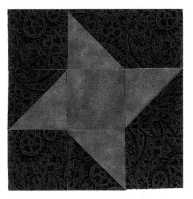

When the same medium-value purple is paired with a light purple background fabric, the resulting block *below* has a higher contrast than the first one because of the difference in values between the purples.

Understanding the relative contrast of color choices is helpful when selecting fabric for your quilt, so you'll achieve the desired contrast between elements.

VISUALIZING CONTRAST

Trying to ignore color and just study contrast is not an easy task. When looking at fabrics in a store or from your fabric stash, try these techniques to see the contrast or value.

Select your fabrics for a project, then perform one or more of these tests to see if you've included enough contrast in the group.

If you need more contrast, substitute lighter or darker fabrics until you have a variety of values.

Try squinting. Closing your eyes slightly limits the amount of light they receive and reduces your perception of color, so contrast becomes more evident.

Use a reducing tool. Purchase a reducing glass or a door peephole.

These tools reduce an image, making color less obvious and contrast more apparent when the fabrics are viewed. Taking instant photographs or looking through a camera also works in this regard.

Look through red cellophane. This technique obliterates the color and allows you to see the continuum of values from light to dark.

Make black and white photocopies. Photocopying completely masks color and can give an indication of contrast between and within pieces of fabric.

QUICK REFERENCE CHART
DETERMINING CONTRAST
LEVELS FOR A QUILT BLOCK

Use the chart *below* and the photo at *right* to assess how changing the contrast between the background and block pieces will affect the block's overall appearance.

For example, if you've chosen a light background and light block pieces (*upper left*), you'll achieve a block with low or no contrast. In comparison, a dark background with light block pieces results in a block with high contrast (*lower left*).

		BLOCK PIECES	
	LIGHT	**MEDIUM**	**DARK**
LIGHT	Low or no contrast	Some contrast	High contrast
MEDIUM	Some contrast	Low or no contrast	Some contrast
DARK	High contrast	Some contrast	Low or no contrast

BACKGROUND

COLOR

After contrast, color or hue becomes the next design element to consider when selecting fabrics for your quilts. Where contrast is an objective quality, color is more subjective and often evokes emotion.

Successfully combining colors takes observation, practice, and a little help from the color wheel. Study the color palettes of quilts, artwork, or fashions that appeal to you. Note the main color and how it is combined with other hues.

USING THE COLOR WHEEL IN QUILTING

Artists in many mediums use the color wheel. With paint the result of blending colors is a little more predictable than with fabric because paint is solid; it doesn't have pattern or texture. Even so, the color wheel is a useful guide in choosing fabric colors.

PRIMARY COLORS

All colors are derived from the three primary colors: red, blue, and yellow. Though you may think of them in terms of color, black, gray, and white are not on the color wheel.

QUICK REFERENCE CHART
PRIMARY AND SECONDARY COLOR COMBINATIONS

PRIMARY COLOR	ANALOGOUS COLORS	COMPLEMENTARY COLOR
	Neighboring colors that coordinate with the primary color. These colors share the primary color, so they'll always work together.	The color opposite a primary color on the color wheel that contains the other two primary colors. A small amount of a color's complement can serve as an accent.
Red	Orange / Violet	Green
Blue	Violet / Green	Orange
Yellow	Green / Orange	Violet

The six-piece color wheel shows the relationship of the primary and secondary colors. Use the information above to understand how analogous and complementary colors work together.

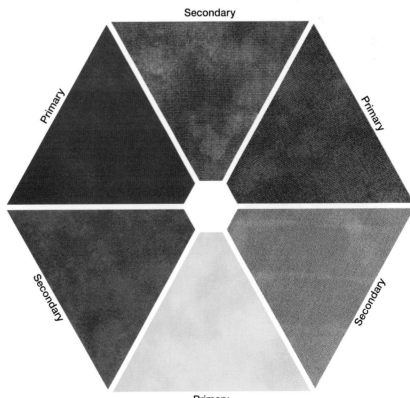

QUICK REFERENCE CHART
12-PIECE COLOR WHEEL (PRIMARY, SECONDARY, AND TERTIARY COLORS)

The middle ring of this color wheel shows the color or hue. The outer ring is the shaded color; black has been added for a darker value of the original color. The inner ring shows the tinted color; white has been added for a lighter value of the original color.

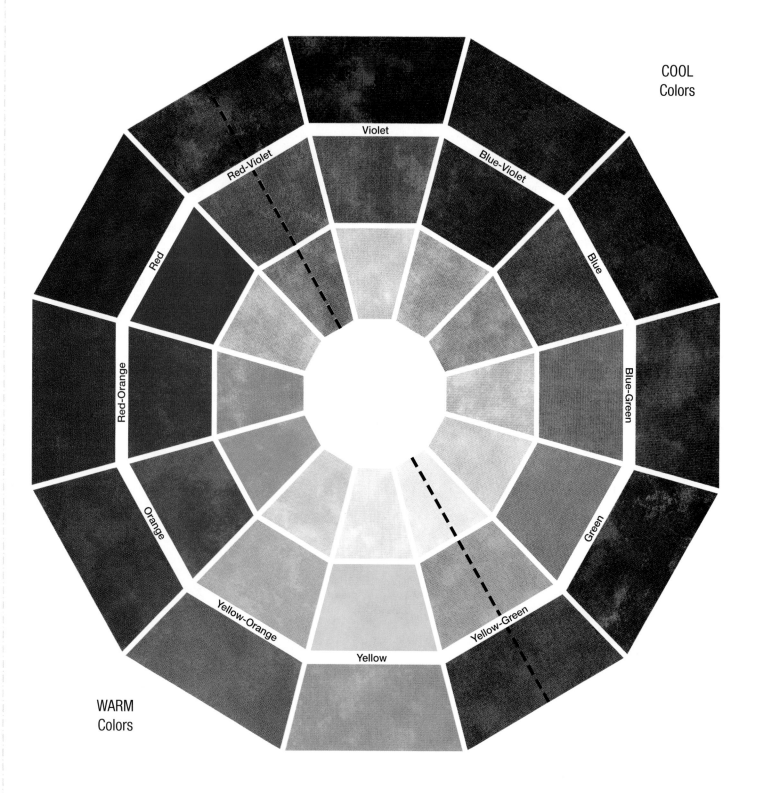

COOL
Colors

WARM
Colors

Fabric & Color

SECONDARY COLORS

When primary colors are mixed in different combinations, the secondary colors of orange, violet, and green are created.

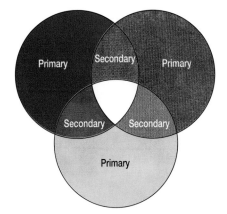

COMPLEMENTARY COLORS

The color that sits opposite a color on the wheel is its complementary color. When combined in equal amounts, complementary colors can vibrate. A popular pair of complementary colors is red and green. True red and true green are a vibrant combination. When they are shaded with a bit of black, they become the calmer colors that are often used for traditional Christmas designs.

A little complementary color can go a long way in adding excitement to a design. For example, include a sprinkle of orange in an otherwise all-blue quilt for a little punch.

TIP: What about neutral colors, such as beige or cream? These colors can be added to one-color and multicolor quilts. In the midst of color, neutral pieces give the eye a place to rest. They spread out competing colors and also add contrast.

QUICK REFERENCE CHART
TINTS AND SHADES OF PRIMARY, SECONDARY, AND TERTIARY COLORS

COLOR	TINT White is added for a lighter color.	SHADE Black is added for a darker color.
Red	Pink	Cranberry
Red-Violet	Magenta	Grape
Violet	Lavender	Eggplant
Blue-Violet	Lilac	Ultramarine
Blue	Periwinkle	Navy
Blue-Green	Aqua	Teal
Green	Seafoam	Forest Green
Yellow-Green	Mint	Olive
Yellow	Daffodil	Gold
Yellow-Orange	Peach	Mustard
Orange	Melon	Cinnamon
Red-Orange	Salmon	Burnt Orange

TERTIARY COLORS

Further divisions of colors are created in a 12-piece color wheel, on *page 2–12*. This wheel shows the primary colors (red, yellow, blue), secondary colors (orange, purple, green), and the tertiary colors, which are a combination of the primary and secondary colors—red-orange, yellow-orange, yellow-green, blue-green, blue-violet, and red-violet.

TINTS AND SHADES

Also shown in the 12-piece color wheel on *page 2–12* are some variations in the colors when they are tinted (white is added) or shaded (black is added), which alters the colors' values. When you consider the infinite amounts of black and white that can be added to make different tints or shades, it's easy to see that the number of colors is limitless.

If the fabric world only had primary, secondary, and tertiary colors, all quilts would be bright and vibrant. Fortunately for those who enjoy a more subtle palette to choose from, fabric designers create additional color options by adding white or black to colors.

TEMPERATURE

Fabrics, like paints, have a warmth, or lack thereof. In a quilt of predominantly cool fabrics (blues), a dash of warmth from orange or yellow can add zip to the quilt.

Fabric & Color

QUICK REFERENCE CHART
SPLIT COMPLEMENT COLOR COMBINATIONS

The split complement combination includes a primary, secondary, or tertiary color and the colors on either side of its complement.

FEATURE FABRIC	SPLIT COMPLEMENTS	
Red	Yellow-Green	Blue-Green
Red-Violet	Yellow	Green
Violet	Yellow-Orange	Yellow-Green
Blue-Violet	Orange	Yellow
Blue	Red-Orange	Yellow-Orange
Blue-Green	Red	Orange
Green	Red-Violet	Red-Orange
Yellow-Green	Red	Violet
Yellow	Red-Violet	Blue-Violet
Yellow-Orange	Violet	Blue
Orange	Blue-Violet	Blue-Green
Red-Orange	Green	Blue

Temperature, like contrast, is relative. The temperature of a color depends on what colors are around it. Look at the color wheel for guidance. Yellow-green and red-violet can be warm or cool depending on who their neighbors are. For example, yellow-green feels cool when used with pure yellow, which is warmer in comparison. The same yellow-green feels warm when paired with greens or blues, which are cooler in comparison. (See the dashed line on the 12-piece color wheel on *page 2–12*. It delineates the warm and cool sections of the color wheel.)

INTENSITY

When looking at a fabric, ask yourself if the color is pure (saturated, brilliant) or muted (grayed, subdued). The answer indicates the fabric's intensity.

Contrast differs from intensity. A dark navy fabric can be brilliant, and a pale yellow can have a low intensity.

In general, use intense colors sparingly, and choose less intense colors for larger areas. Intense colors will appear to come forward, while less intense colors will recede.

Intensity is also a relative characteristic; it changes according to the fabrics that surround it. Observe in the photo *above right* how intense the small red square looks when placed on the larger

TIP: The color wheel can help you classify a particular fabric, allowing you to select additional fabrics and colors to combine with it for a quilt.

black square; it pops out from the background.

When the same red square is placed on the larger white square, it appears to recede.

When combined with the muted gray square, the intensity of the red seems to lessen.

COMBINING COLORS

Remember that the color wheels and charts presented in this book are created from pictures of solid or marbled fabrics. The colors are bright and pure. Fabrics you choose may have similar colors, but could be influenced by pattern and additional colors in the fabric. Use these charts only as a guide.

Study individual fabrics and note their color combinations. Often the fabric manufacturer has printer's dots on the selvage that show the colors used to create the fabric design. Replicating these colors exactly can create a flat quilt, but

QUICK REFERENCE CHART
TRIAD COLOR COMBINATIONS

The triad combination uses three primary, secondary, or tertiary colors that are equidistant on the color wheel. There are four possible triad combinations, but your choice of tints, shades, and intensities within each is unlimited. Each triad shown below includes an example of colors that would work well together in a three-color quilt.

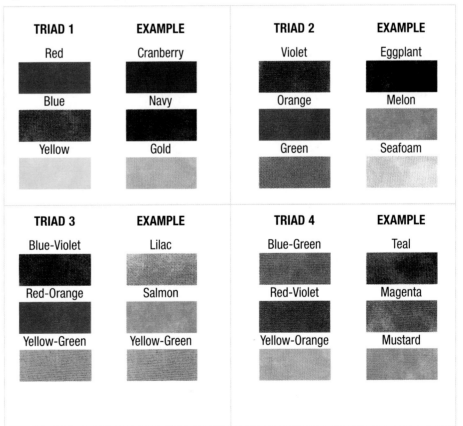

using tints and shades of the colors, as well as a variety of intensities (pure colors versus muted, grayed colors) and temperatures (warm versus cool colors) can enhance a design (see *pages 2–14* and *2–15* for more information on temperature and intensity).

Consider the following guidelines and types of color combinations when choosing fabrics for your quilt.

MONOCHROMATIC

While a monochromatic quilt uses a single color, every color has tinted and shaded variations. If you're interested in composing a single-color quilt, refer to the Quick Reference Chart for Tints and Shades of Primary, Secondary, and Tertiary Colors on *page 2–13* for possible color combinations in planning a monochromatic quilt. Choose one of the primary, secondary, or tertiary colors, then consider including all of the tints through shades of that color. A one-color quilt is most successful when the fabrics' designs, textures, and contrasts vary.

TIP: Where does brown fit in? Brown is not on the color wheel because it has all the colors in it. Use brown when you don't want to add another color but need some type of contrast or transition.

SPLIT COMPLEMENTS

A split complement color scheme includes a primary, secondary, or tertiary color and the colors on either side of its complement.

For example, if you have a violet fabric and want its split complement colors, looking at the 12-Piece Color Wheel on *page 2–12* shows they would be yellow-orange and yellow-green. These are the colors on either side of violet's complementary color, yellow—directly across on the color wheel. If these pure colors seem strong, consider that violet, yellow-orange, and yellow-green could be eggplant, olive, and mustard, three warm and mellow colors. The Quick Reference Chart for Split Complement Color Combinations on *page 2–14* can help you devise a split complement color scheme.

ANALOGOUS COLOR COMBINATIONS

Think of analogous colors as neighbors. If you desire a quilt of this type, select a favorite fabric as your feature fabric and find its closest companion on the color wheel. Pull the remaining fabrics for your quilt from the neighboring, or adjacent, colors.

For example, if the feature fabric is a green, then pick a variety of light and dark fabrics in yellow-green, yellow, blue-green, and blue. This is one of the safest palettes to work with, but it can look dull if the fabrics don't have some interest in their patterns and variety in contrast.

TRIAD COMBINATIONS

A triad combination—three colors that are equidistant on the color wheel—results in a harmonious quilt. There are four triad combinations from which to choose, and you can select from an unlimited number of tints, shades, and intensities within those colors. The Quick Reference Chart for Triad Color Combinations on *page 2–15* shows the four triad combinations and a color combination example for each.

TETRAD COMBINATIONS

A tetrad combination—four colors that are equidistant on the color wheel—is another way to select quilt fabrics. There are three combinations from which to choose. Again, you can select from an unlimited number of tints, shades, and intensities within those colors. The Quick Reference Chart for Tetrad Color Combinations, *opposite*, shows the three tetrad combinations and a color combination example for each.

POLYCHROMATIC COMBINATIONS

Polychromatic, or multicolor, combinations are often scrap quilts—those composed of myriad fabrics in a wide range of colors and textures. Varying contrast, intensity, and temperature helps tie these quilts together (see *pages 2–14* and *2–15* for more information on temperature and intensity). Adding neutral fabrics to the mix provides balance among colors that might otherwise compete for attention.

QUICK REFERENCE CHART
TETRAD COLOR COMBINATIONS

The tetrad combination uses four primary, secondary, or tertiary colors that are equidistant on the color wheel. There are three possible tetrad combinations, but your choice of tints, shades, and intensities within each is unlimited. Each tetrad shown below includes an example of colors that would work well together in a four-color quilt.

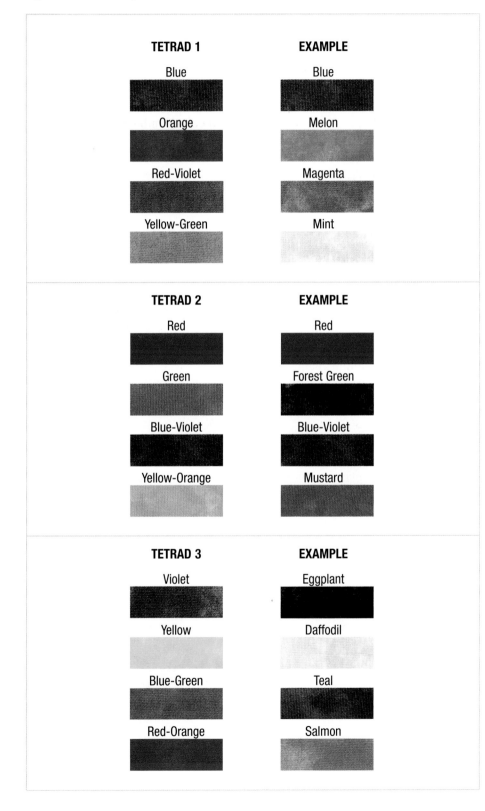

TETRAD 1	EXAMPLE
Blue	Blue
Orange	Melon
Red-Violet	Magenta
Yellow-Green	Mint

TETRAD 2	EXAMPLE
Red	Red
Green	Forest Green
Blue-Violet	Blue-Violet
Yellow-Orange	Mustard

TETRAD 3	EXAMPLE
Violet	Eggplant
Yellow	Daffodil
Blue-Green	Teal
Red-Orange	Salmon

The third element that affects quilt design is the character of the fabrics, the features that change how each one works in a block or an overall quilt top. Prints may contain the same hues, for example, but may look different when placed in a block. One may be an elegant floral reproduction fabric, while the other is perhaps a stripe or a conversation print of animals. Consider each fabric's character when making selection decisions.

OVERALL CHARACTER

Color, contrast, and print style aside, fabrics have overall characteristics that should be taken into account.

Scale

Scale refers to the relative size of the print's elements. Quilts benefit from a range—small, medium and large— in scale.

Small-scale prints will look as though they're solid, but will contribute additional color and add visual texture.

Medium-scale prints tend to be quilters' favorites because they are easy to use and most readily

available. Even when cut or viewed from a distance, they tend to retain their design.

Large-scale prints are visually appealing on the bolt but require a little extra care when incorporating them into a design. Test large-scale prints with a window template to see what colors or parts will appear when cut into smaller pieces. (See *page 2–4* for information on making window templates.) Use care because a large-scale print can appear fragmented if used for small pieces within a block. They are best in borders and setting blocks.

Mood

Is the print busy or calm? Is the fabric elegant and formal or playful and lively? Coordinate fabric moods to convey the desired effect.

PRINT STYLE

Variations in Contrast

When selecting fabrics, be sure to look for variety in contrast, or values, within each color family. This adds more life to a quilt. Consider that an individual fabric can have contrast within itself—a red print, for example, that has areas

of pink and burgundy—which brings interest to a monochromatic block or quilt.

Solid and Tone-On-Tone Prints

Solid-color fabrics or tone-on-tone prints (prints that look like solids when viewed from a distance) help set areas of the quilt apart from other prints or linear designs. Tone-on-tone prints add subtle visual texture without competing for the eye's attention.

Striped, Checked, or Plaid Fabric

Available in structured designs or

wavy lines, stripes, checks, and plaids can add pizzazz to blocks or units. Try them as sashing or small inner borders.

Stripes also make fun binding. For example, cutting a striped fabric on the bias can produce the effect of a barber-pole stripe around the edge of your quilt.

Black-and-White Fabric

Don't overlook black-and-white fabrics when shopping for color. Sometimes such a print can be the answer if you want to add some punch to your quilt design.

Large-Scale Prints

Large-scale prints, such as floral motifs, leaves, and paisleys, are often used as feature or focus fabrics. Use a window template to determine how a large-scale print might look when cut into smaller pieces. (See *page 2–4* for information on making window templates.) Purchase additional yardage if the fabric is going to be used as a border. Using a large print in both the quilt center and border helps bring unity to a quilt top.

Conversation or Novelty Prints

These prints depict themes, including sewing tools, holiday

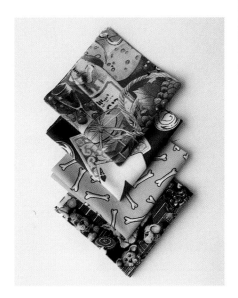

symbols, corporate logos, and even hobbies. If you're having difficulty working a favorite conversation print into a quilt top, use it for the backing instead. Or, if you're using it as the main motif in a block, try fussy-cutting it to center the desired area. (See Chapter 5—Cutting for information on fussy cutting.)

Reproduction Fabrics

Whether you're choosing fabrics for a Civil War-era quilt or a reproduction 1930s design, there are many fabric collections available

that re-create prints from bygone eras. The color and design elements of these reproductions may be such that it's easiest to combine them with other reproduction fabrics from the same collection or era.

Variety in fabrics results in an eye-catching quilt.

VARIETY CHECKLIST

Ask yourself these questions to determine if you've achieved variety in your selection of quilt fabrics.

Contrast
- Is there a variety of light-, medium-, and dark-value fabrics for the blocks, appliqués, and the overall quilt top?

Color
- Have I selected colors according to a certain color scheme or grouping of color families—primary, secondary, complementary, tertiary, etc.?
- Are there shades and tints within color families represented in the fabrics chosen?
- Do the fabric intensities work well together?

Character
- Have I chosen a variety of print styles?
- Have I included small-, medium-, and large-scale prints?
- Is the mood of the fabrics appropriate for the quilt I plan to make?

Abstract or Painterly Fabrics

Batiks and hand-dyed fabrics can be great choices when you're looking for subtle changes in color and texture, such as where you want a transition between colors.

TIP: Having extra fabrics on hand when working on a project opens up opportunities for substitutions and the additional variety quilts often need. Buy fabrics you like in the colors you enjoy. Working with fabrics you enjoy will help you maintain enthusiasm throughout the project, thus achieving the best overall results.

AUDITIONING FABRICS

Combining fabrics successfully may take experimentation, patience, and experience. Understanding the basics of contrast, color, and character will take some of the trial and error out of putting fabrics together.

Use the variety checklist on *page 2–19* while making fabric choices for your quilt. The questions may help you determine what, if anything, is missing from a design.

Distance

One of the best ways to tell if your fabric combination will work is to step back from it. Fabrics that don't appear to work when viewed up close may be perfect from a distance, where you can see a fabric's contribution to the whole. Remember that each piece is just a fraction of the total finished product.

TIP: Why Scrap Quilts Work. Scrap quilts make the ultimate statement concerning the impact of contrast. It doesn't matter what colors are used in a scrap quilt, but rather how the pieces contrast with one another.

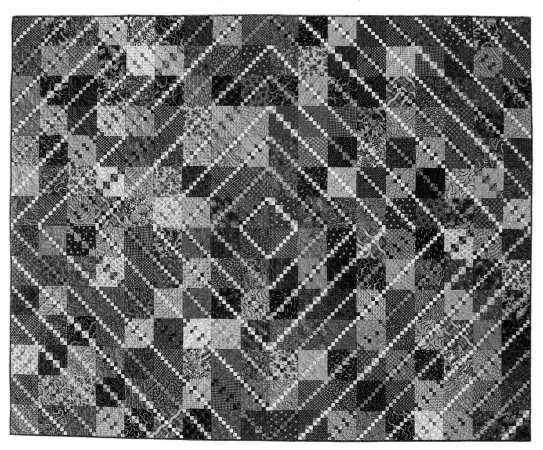

Color Photocopy

Photocopy your fabric choices on a color copier to test your options. (See Chapter 3—Planning Pieced Blocks for more information on testing fabric choices using photocopies.)

Design Wall

Having a surface to vertically lay out fabric choices can help you visualize how they will look in a quilt. For a permanent or portable design wall, cover the surface of foam-core board with a napped material, such as flannel, that will hold small pieces in place for viewing. Some quilters use the flannel back of oilcloth for a design wall, rolling it up between projects or hanging one in front of the other to view different quilts.

TROUBLESHOOTING TIPS

Having trouble choosing fabrics for your quilt?
Use these ideas to help find solutions to your color dilemmas.

IF YOU DON'T KNOW WHERE TO START
- Read quilt books, studying the designs and noting those you like best.
- Join a quilt guild. You'll gain inspiration and garner advice from fellow quilters.
- Identify a favorite feature fabric and use it as a starting point for choosing others.
- Study color combinations in favorite items.

IF YOU LIKE A PATTERN BUT NOT ITS COLORS
- Study color combinations in favorite articles of clothing.
- Look at home decorating magazines for possible color inspiration.

IF FABRICS CHOSEN HAVE NO COLOR CONTINUITY
- Replace some of the stronger colors with their muted versions.
- Try adding a complementary color.
- Choose a feature fabric to use in the blocks and borders to unify the overall design.
- Add neutrals or less intense colors to give the eye a place to rest.

IF CERTAIN PIECES ARE TOO DOMINANT
- Look at each piece and determine whether there is high contrast within the piece or with the pieces around it. Decrease the contrast accordingly.

IF BLOCK PIECES BLEND TOGETHER SO THAT THE DESIGN IS LOST
- Check the values of the fabrics involved and substitute fabrics in colors with higher contrast.

FABRIC SHOPPING CHECKLIST

Photocopy this checklist and take it with you when you're buying fabric for a quilt. Attach fabric swatches to the checklist as a reminder of what you've already purchased and to be certain you get enough variety in color, contrast, and character. (See Chapter 5—Cutting, Chapter 9—Assembling the Quilt Top, and Chapter 10—Batting & Backing for information on determining the yardages needed.)

PATTERN NAME _____   COLOR SCHEME _____

Batting Type _____ Size Needed _____   Sketch of quilt top (or attach pattern)

FEATURE FABRIC 1   Yardage Needed_____

Fabric 2	Fabric 3	Fabric 4	Fabric 5
Yardage Needed_____	Yardage Needed_____	Yardage Needed_____	Yardage Needed_____

Border Fabric 1	Border Fabric 2	Binding Fabric	Backing Fabric
Yardage Needed_____	Yardage Needed_____	Yardage Needed_____	Yardage Needed_____

Fabric & Color

Planning
Pieced
Blocks

TABLE OF CONTENTS
Chapter 3—Planning Pieced Blocks

PLANNING PIECED BLOCKS

QUILTS AND QUILT DESIGNS OFTEN ARISE FROM A SINGLE BLOCK OR GROUPING OF UNITS. Understanding how blocks are created can help you dissect a quilt design, thus allowing you to duplicate its elements. Learning more about combining block elements also may enable you to design original quilt blocks.

COMBINING GEOMETRIC SHAPES INTO UNITS

Individual geometric shapes and their combinations are the foundation of every quilt block. On the following pages, several common shapes are shown. Study the different shapes in blocks. Knowing the shapes will make cutting and piecing easier to understand.

The term *unit* is used frequently in block design and pattern directions. Units are composed of at least two shapes sewn together. In this chapter, the shapes that combine to make a unit are

WHAT IS A BLOCK?
The majority of quilts are built on a basic unit called a block. Most commonly these block units are square, but they can also be rectangular, triangular, or another shape such as a hexagon. A single block style or several block styles may be used in a single quilt.

illustrated. For specific instructions on piecing methods for these units, see Chapter 6—Hand Piecing or Chapter 7—Machine Piecing.

Many blocks are built from common units such as the triangle-square and Flying Geese. Knowing how a block is divided into units can help you determine how a quilt is put together and allows efficiency in piecing.

SQUARES
Whether it is a simple setting block, the foundation for an appliqué block, or part of a unit, the square is one of the most common geometric shapes used in quilt designs.

Four-Patch Unit
Four equal-size squares sewn in two rows of two result in a Four-Patch unit. This unit acts as a block in some quilts.

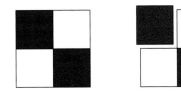

Nine-Patch Unit
Nine equal-size squares sewn in three rows of three form a Nine-Patch block or a unit within a block. Often these units are composed of two alternating colors.

RECTANGLES
Rectangles can be combined into square units.

Two- and Three-Bar Units
Depending on the size of your rectangles and the desired size of your finished square, any number of bars can be used to create a square.

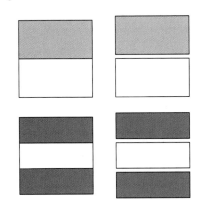

Alternating the direction of those squares produces a Rail Fence block.

TIP: When you're ready to plan your own blocks, use colored pencils and the graph paper on *pages 3–17 to 3–23.*